**What people are saying about
The Ideal Marketing Company...**

"It is so refreshing to hear new and exciting ideas about how you can utilise marketing tools in your own business."
- LEANNE AYRIS, Harvey Middleton Ltd

"If you are passionate about growing your business fast, then get the Ideal Marketing Company involved. Their creative low cost marketing ideas are ideal for any small business keen to expand on a limited budget."
- HAYDN YOUNG, Gaia Active

"[The Ideal Marketing Company's] knowledge and expertise has assisted in the growth of our company. The advice, guidance and techniques they suggested in our marketing have helped us attract new customers and make sure we were maximising the retention of our existing customers."
- DAVID CROWTHER, Andrew Bourne & Co

"Coming from a marketing background, I have been sceptical about the services offered by other marketing companies. The Ideal Marketing Company has totally changed my view... with real tangible results. I've become more focused, more productive and believe it or not actually saved money! I recommend Alastair and his team at every opportunity - he really can turn a good business into a great business."
- LYNN LEWIS, Jamie Lewis Residential

"Alastair has a knack for finding creative, cost effective ways of marketing your company. Ideas that are do-able by yourself and that produce results."

   – GARRY ASTON, Caged Fish

"We have worked together on a number of initiatives and Alastair is a real breath of fresh air. He is constantly creative and comes up with many innovative ideas. He is also very positive and aware of the needs of small businesses."

   – ANDREW SEAWARD, To Market

"Precision Recruitment has been working with Alastair for a few years and have found his infectious energy and ideas and campaigns from concept through to implementation of massive value to our business... [he] has helped us considerably to increase our presence in today's increasingly competitive market place."

   – SCOTT LYDON, Precision Recruitment

"I have heard Alastair from The Ideal Marketing Company speak about marketing and business on several occasions and always found him articulate and inspiring. I would have no hesitation in recommending him to others."

   – ELOISE SHELTON, Vanilla Recruitment

...now, in this book, he shares his tips, secrets and insights into successful marketing with you.

The Marketing Launchpad

The six key areas of marketing
to lift your business to new heights

Alastair Campbell

MOSAÏQUEPRESS

Published by

MOSAÏQUE PRESS

6 Clarence Terrace

Warwick Street

Leamington Spa

CV32 5LD

www.mosaïquepress.co.uk

Cover design by Paul Johnson
www.pjd-uk.com

ISBN 978-1-906852-05-4

Dedicated to Helen, Robbie and Ben who make all the long hours and hard work worthwhile.

Contents

Reaching out to your customer

Alastair Campbell has written this book to guide you through the process of marketing your business. Most people I coach in small businesses believe they don't know 'how to' do certain important things like marketing and selling. But the 'how to' is never what's missing. What's missing is really the 'want to'... the deep, single-minded desire to be a dramatic success.

Once you get that 'want to' in place, the 'how to' will show up everywhere... like this book right here.

For a small business, the right marketing can launch you. But it has to be right. It has to connect with your prospective customers and clients, and connect in ways that actually begin the sales process.

Becoming passionate and knowledgeable about strong and effective marketing is the first (and most necessary) step to business success. We live in a weakened age... people are looking for handouts, bail-outs, government assistance, and all kinds of 'help.' However, true and rapid success comes from a mindset of self help, a mindset of self-reliance and a mindset of business power. Successful businesses are created. They don't just 'happen' to people who catch a lucky break with a hot product or service. Your marketing is the most important part of that creation because it is the part that reaches out to your customer, takes him by the hand, and walks him through your doors.

Make it something you know and care about. Start with this book.

Steve Chandler
Author of *The Story of You*
www.stevechandler.com

Introduction

Is your business ready for lift-off?

This book reveals the six most powerful marketing areas that you need to understand to launch your business into a new orbit. If you decide to ignite all six, you will be giving your business the chance to lift off like never before.

The ideas and examples in these chapters are not dry academic theories. Each one is based on the real life experience from my own career or from one of my clients' successes. Used properly and in a sustained manner, the information in each section is capable of doubling or tripling your business over time.

Many of the examples here are from my clients who are mainly based in and around the Midlands in England. But these ideas would apply equally to your company, whether it is in Elgin in Scotland or Emmetsburg in Iowa.

You almost certainly have used some elements of marketing in your business in the past. However, if you are like most people, you will have used marketing in a reactive way. When the phone goes quiet, the order book dries up and people stop returning your calls, it's a prompt to start marketing. Unfortunately, for many by that point it may be too late. The time to start consistently marketing your business is right now – even if you are busy with incoming enquiries.

Marketing isn't a switch that you can turn on and off. Think of your business as a rocket on the launch pad waiting to lift off. Everything seems to be there – the astronaut sitting in the capsule (that's you, by the way) waiting for something to happen. But unless you know how to market your business in a cost-effective way, it's like building the rocket – but leaving off the engines.

The six sections of this book are the marketing engines that will enable your business to lift off to new heights. They are powerful, efficient and well tested. You are not being asked to take a dangerous risk, in fact quite the opposite. These marketing ideas will actually reduce the risks of failure because they have worked for so many business owners already.

Despite what people will tell you, it doesn't have to be expensive and it doesn't have to be a gamble. While it is true that there is nothing certain about the results you will achieve, there are plenty of shortcuts that you can take that will dramatically increase the likelihood that you will succeed. These ideas often don't need to cost any more; more often that not they will actually cost you the same as what you currently spend – or less.

For example, if you send out 1,000 direct mail letters that use the wrong language, the wrong ideas, the wrong tone of voice and the wrong headline, you may get a 0.5 per cent response rate. That means that you would have to post out 200 letters for one person to reply. And that person might not actually buy from you – only ask you for more information about what you do.

But imagine that you could change the response rate to five

per cent – which is most certainly possible. That means you only need to post out 20 letters to receive one reply. You have improved your response rate 10-fold. That is quite a difference just by using the right words, never mind the saving on stamps and printing. Now imagine that increase in response week in, week out. Does that make you want to smile?

I was asked to run a direct mail campaign for a company a few years back. This company had been writing to people week after week for three years (which is commendable). However, they had not received a single enquiry (as far as they knew) from anybody they had written to. By my calculations, their letters had gone to 15,600 companies over that three-year period and they did not know of one enquiry or one sale that it had generated.

By writing a new letter and taking a new tack the following week, I generated 20 enquiries, more than 50 per cent of which resulted in meetings, sales or both. The MD kept saying: "If only we had done this sooner."

My letter hadn't cost any extra to post out; it just used a simple idea that I'll tell you about later in this book. I didn't invent it, I just copied a proven marketing concept. Now it's your turn to copy and adapt it from me.

While we are on the subject of copying ideas, do you know how to sell more oranges? Unless you are a market trader or an interior designer, you might not know the answer to this one. But it is also a principle that many people use and one that the *Blackadder* and *Love Actually* writer Richard Curtis understands all too well.

The best way to bring out the impact of a colour is to place it beside the 'opposite' colour. And according to the colour wheel, the opposite of orange is a purple/purple blue combination. That means if you want your oranges to stand out more, to look more 'orange' and therefore to sell more, you should place them on a blue or purple tray.

The principle of colour contrast is understood by sign designers who often will use contrasting colours to make signs really stand out against each other. Richard Curtis understands this principle but in his case it is making comedy and heartache appear side by side when he co-ordinates the fund raising for *Comic Relief*. It's the contrast that makes each part stand out more than they would if it was all funny or all sad.

Now direct mail might not work for your company. And there may not be a way of using the old market trader's trick of shifting extra oranges if you are an accountant. In fact, there is no single way to best market every business. Each company has its own strong points, and in all likelihood its weaker ones. While one company has a product that will sell well via direct mail, another is perfectly suited to the Internet. Another company may find that its products are very newsworthy, while yet another finds that an extensive colour brochure is its best sales tool.

So, before we start this book, I want you to know that I don't for one second expect you to implement each and every idea that it contains.

That said, most companies are missing out on a huge wealth of marketing opportunities. When I ask in my seminars how many people regularly work on some marketing activity each week, fewer than 25 per cent put their hand up. Around 10 per cent have sent out a news release in the past year. While more than 60 per cent of companies tell me they have a website, fewer than 10 per cent have any way of updating any part of that site.

In fact, most will say that they rely on just one or two ways of generating business. This might be 'word of mouth' or relying on passing trade. What they are saying is that marketing is a bit beyond them and that therefore they have put the future growth of their company – and therefore the future of their children – in the hands of strangers and the whim that they might decide to buy something.

If you have only one main method of generating new business, that's like having one leg to support your table. It's perilous at the best of times, but if anything goes wrong with that one leg, you will soon be eating your dinner off the carpet.

The good news is that there is plenty of practical, low-budget stuff that you can do starting today to generate interest in what you do. Whether you are a fish monger or a landscape gardener, this book contains straightforward ideas that can be quickly introduced.

So here is what I suggest you do:

First of all, when you read this book, do so with an open mind. Ask yourself: "What ideas are contained within this chapter that could TRANSFORM my company?" When I used to stuff hundreds of direct mail letters for a former employer and then take them to the post box on a Saturday morning I would think to myself, "perhaps one of these letters is going to result in a multi-million pound order for the company." In truth, several of them did, but that's another story.

So, don't skip a chapter or read it thinking, "there is nothing in this section for me." I can promise you that if that is your attitude, you will be correct – there won't be anything in that chapter for you.

Secondly, scribble and make notes as much as you like. Don't treat this book as if it were a library book (unless of course it is a library book). Underline sections you find helpful and highlight phrases that you want to re-read. Don't worry about making a mess. Just try to make it easier for yourself when you come back to a section in a few months.

And thirdly and finally, adapt and try these ideas out for yourself. They really work. I've seen them produce results time and time again for clients and for friends and for companies big and small. If they have worked for so many others, there is a good chance that at least some of them will work for you.

However, just like that rocket sitting on the launchpad, they won't do you any good unless someone ignites them – pushes the red button – and that is where you come in. It won't happen by itself.

Just reading these ideas won't bring in a single penny to your company. You need to take these ideas on board and start taking action if you want your business to really lift off.

I'm pleased to say that a client went from being almost broke to generating more than £5,000 a week by trying out one of the direct mail ideas. That's one of literally hundreds of examples I can give you of people who have used these ideas to maintain or turn around the success of their company.

If you are serious about growing your company but have a small amount of available time and a limited budget, I hope you agree with me that this book will work for you. It's based on real examples, it's practical and it can be dipped into as a refresher whenever you need it.

Remember, these ideas are pretty well universal. They apply whether your business is well established or a start-up. In fact, whatever industry you are in and whatever success (or lack of it) you have had until now, the six key areas that this book reveals will make a dramatic difference if you apply them consistently.

I hope you are as excited as I am about the possibilities that they could bring to your business. Just one of these chapters properly applied could be the turning point that you are looking for.

There is no right way to read this book. If you are halfway through a section and an idea strikes you, you don't have to complete the chapter. You can do that idea straight away. Similarly, you don't need to read the chapters in the order in which they are laid out. There is some logic here in suggesting that you would sort out your branding (Chapter 1) before you would look into your direct mail (Chapter 4), but that's not always the case. If you are happy with your brand as it is, but need some quick orders through the door this week, then by all means start reading about direct mail first. For best results though, I would suggest the following:

- Buy a wall chart (like the ones used to plan holidays) where you can put up your key promotional times, events, campaign themes etc.
- For each chapter in the book, make a list of the activities that you can apply in your company.
- Decide if you are the best person to take on the activity. Is

there somebody else within your organisation who has the skills, or are you better off finding outside help?

- Make a start on the area that you think is likely to generate the best return in the short term. Do something that is likely to generate results quickly.

From now on, you are going to measure how successful your marketing activity is, so get some pads printed up with a space to write down the name of the caller, their e-mail, phone number and where they are calling from. As with most things, it is easier if you have a system in place rather than relying on an individual to remember. So make it a policy that everybody who is near a phone has one of these pads. You can either photocopy the page opposite or use it as a template to create you own pads.

You don't have to be a rocket scientist to work out that doing more of what already is working for you will see the growth of your business really lift off.

Oh – one final thing. Please let me know how you get on. If you use an idea from here, if you have tried something similar or if you have a suggestion, then please let me know. I always love to hear about success stories and who knows, you might even get a mention in the next edition of the book!

Alastair Campbell
alastair@idealmarketingcompany.com

* NEW LEAD SHEET * IMPORTANT *

Date _____

Name _____

Company_____

Phone _____

e-mail_____

They heard about us via:

Website_____

Direct mail _____

Flyer _____

Newspaper advert _____

Directory _____

Recommendation _____

PR _____

Other_____

Orders /quote /request details:

Pre Launch Checklist

☐ Make a monthly checklist to see what marketing is working best for you and WHERE, and if you find one area that stands out from the others (using the real results that you are measuring rather than guesswork) then work out how you can do more of it.

☐ As you get used to finding out what works best for you, start to increase your spend on those activities, and reduce or eliminate spending on the areas that don't work for you. That way, even by keeping your advertising and marketing budget the same, you can increase its effectiveness by between two and 10 times.

☐ Start looking at the way your competitors, other local companies and big brands advertise. Do their messages connect with you? Do they make you want to buy from them? Who are they targeting with their messages? Is there something that you can learn or copy from what they are doing?

☐ What are the different elements of your business? If you are a restaurant, you might want to break it down into breakfasts, lunches, dinners, snacks, special events and functions. What are you doing to promote each activity? Can you break it down into regular patterns of activities so that each area receives some attention?

☐ If you use a daily 'to do' list, start writing down one area of marketing (even if it's a small one) every day.

☐ Get into the habit of asking other business owners what marketing activity works for them. It's a good ice breaker at networking events and will give you some ideas for what WORKS as opposed to what you might THINK works.

Chapter 1

Building your brand

• Definition of brand • The key attributes of good branding • The history of early brands • The nine areas of branding • The importance of longevity in creating a successful brand •

> You don't have to be a global company to recognise the importance of branding.

Some people think that branding is just for huge companies with millions to burn. I hope that by the end of this chapter you will realise that branding, when it is done properly, can not only enhance your sales, but over time it can make your company worth considerably more if you decide to sell it. So don't think that branding is necessarily an expensive vanity thing. It is a way of making a clear statement to your customers about what you stand for and why they should buy from you.

In this chapter, we will look at aspects of branding including creating a company logo and ethos and how you can apply these ideas to your business, or to products within your business. But is it really necessary? Isn't branding just for the big boys?

In fact creating a brand will help your business to:

- send a clear benefit-led message
- confirm and enhance your credibility
- connect your target prospects emotionally
- motivate the buyer
- cement user loyalty.

No matter how long you have been going – whether you run an inherited family firm or a fresh start-up – branding has an important part to play in growing your business that is not to be overlooked. Even if you have been getting it wrong in the past, it is not too late to change.

And people do get it wrong – even some major players. When I worked for a large London advertising agency, one of the many paradoxes I noticed was the way that brands were handled. If a campaign worked well, the brand manager would be head-hunted and the first thing his successor would do was change the campaign to make a name for himself – thus often reducing the value of the brand. Of course if a campaign failed, the brand manager would often be fired and a new manager brought in who would of course rebrand, thus (more often than not) reducing the value of the brand – and ultimately the business.

This went on all the time – the trade magazines were full of stories about people coming and going and the constant hiring and firing at agencies. I think this merry-go-round is one of the reasons why branding goes awry and is cut short so often before

great brands are created. Campaigns with potential are stopped
dead in their tracks.

Defining branding

First of all, what is a brand? At the one-day seminar I run, we
talk about how the term's origins in antiquity refer to the act of
placing a permanent mark of ownership on property. An example
from the more recent past is the way ranchers on vast open
grazing identified their cattle. They would take a red-hot branding
iron with a unique pattern or series of letters and press it onto the
hind quarter of a cow where it left a permanent mark. The brand
mark's individual shape meant that the particular animal was
theirs. More humane forms of branding livestock are used now. It
is a way of identifying what is yours in the absence of boundaries
or other forms of demarcation. It makes it clear what is yours by
use of a visual symbol.

A more useful definition in this context of marketing is that
branding is a trade name given to a product or service. It is a
way of identifying something as recognisable and distinctive
from other products. It is a way of creating something that is
proprietary. It belongs to you, rather than any other company.
A brand can either be the company (Kellogg's) or the products
of the company (Kellogg's Corn Flakes, Frosties, All-Bran etc).

In my view, branding should have all or most of these features:

● It will have a clear benefit-led message. Somewhere in the
  brand, there'll be a message that will offer a clear benefit
  to the customers at whom you are aiming your product.

- It confirms and enhances the credibility of your business rather than taking it away. If branding is about price and being cheap, that is okay because that is part of the core message that you are aiming to get across. So it confirms and enhances that credibility.

- It connects to your target prospects. This is significant as a brand can be incredibly important for some people. Take something like Harley Davidson. For me personally, not being a motorbike enthusiast, it doesn't mean much. But ask a Harley Davidson enthusiast (like my next door neighbour) and they will tell you about the importance of the brand... you even see people who have Harley Davidson tattoos on their arms, it is that important to them. That is one brand that definitely connects with its target audience on an emotional level.

- It motivates the buyer to come back to you for more or to share that information with other people, being enthusiastic with other people about what you're selling.

- It encourages user loyalty. People swear by a particular brand. It creates, in their mind, a belief that they want to be associated with it. Apple is a good example. One of the huge branding successes of late is the iPhone. Some iPhone users talk about their phone with such pride you would think that they had invented it.

Origins of brands

The first brand, according to the *Guinness Book of World Records*, was Lyle's Golden Syrup, made by Tate and Lyle. It was created and registered in 1885 and, interestingly, a tin of Lyle's Golden Syrup is virtually unchanged (apart from some health and safety legislation and the list of ingredients on the back) from when it was first put on the shelves well over 100 years ago. It has that distinctive golden and green colour which hasn't changed over the years.

If you look closely at the tin, you will see it has the decomposing corpse of a lion around which are bees creating honey. The message that "from the strength came sweetness" is taken from the Bible – Abram Lyle, the company founder, was a devout Presbyterian. It is quite unusual, to say the least. Most people would have long since changed the design, but it is distinctive and has lasted for a very long time. Here are some of the qualities that this brand has:

- As a product it is distinctive. At a time when black treacle was a popular product, they created a 'golden' syrup with a distinctive taste and colour. It stands out from the competition It is different from products on the shelves now, and it was certainly different from products at the time it was created.
- It has a memorable and distinctive message.
- It has a clear visual symbol: in this case the green and gold tin as well as the lion used in the logo.
- It has a very clear position in the market with an identified audience. It has made a niche for itself within the market place.
- It is increasing the value of the business. This is something we'll look at later as branding is all about increasing the value of business.

- It can act as a branding device across a number of products. If you create successful brands, they can be used to launch sub-brands or similar brands in different areas.
- Finally, (and Golden Syrup doesn't really have this final point) it positions itself as having a clear and distinct advantage to the consumer.

These are the seven qualities that help create a good brand. A great brand does not normally have all seven qualities, but a poor brand will often have none of them. Let's have a look at each of these areas in more detail and see how many of the most famous examples of successful branding illustrate these points.

Create a hook

Do you stand out from the competition? When working with clients, I often make creating a hook one of the first projects we work on. Sometimes it can be visual element and sometimes it is an intellectual idea that you can 'hang' other elements onto.

When I was setting up the Marketing Mentor programme, I created the idea of 'cogs' for each element of marketing. Put together a series of cogs and you create a marketing 'machine' to help power your company forward. It is a simple visual metaphor that makes a simple point.

When working with my client the Heart of the Shires – a shopping village in Northamptonshire – I was asked to re-create the branding of the centre. The units had been there for around 20 years, based in old Victorian converted farm buildings. When I started to work with them, Heart of the Shires had some elements they wanted to keep, like the name and shade of green that was used within some of the signage. But they were looking at repositioning themselves in the marketplace. The first question we asked was 'How is a visit to Heart of the Shires different from a visit to the average High Street?' The answer to that question formed the basis of the re-branding we created.

For a start, they didn't have large national shopping chain stores. Instead, they had small independent shops. So the experience of shoppers was more friendly and personal. They told us it was like travelling back to a bygone era of service. So we came up with the end line 'Shopping as it should be'. Everything about the site was evocative of old-fashioned values and ideas about quality and service. Now any events that are held on the site are linked to this theme: a Victorian themed balloon race is an example. The image we created for their logo has a Victorian gentleman with a hat on and a lady wearing a bonnet. Two of the colours that are associated with the idea of quality are gold and green, so these were used on the logo.

How do you create a hook for your company? Look at what makes you special and different? Do you have qualities that are different and desirable? Look at what is different about what you do compared to other companies in the market. Is there a visual metaphor for that?

Creating a memorable and distinctive message

In an age of mass production, intense competition and instant gratification, identifying something that is distinctive about your company or its products is a challenge. Look at the way cars are marketed. In a sector where arguably there are more similarities than differences, many manufacturers will exploit particular strengths in design, real or imagined. For example:

- Volvo = safety. For years, that was the message Volvo's advertising put across. Now I'm not an expert on car safety, but I think most modern cars are pretty safe. I'm not sure if a Volvo is safer than the average car, but in my mind I can't help associating Volvo with that image.
- VW = reliability. Again, in my experience, most modern cars are very reliable. Volkswagens are probably no more reliable than other cars, but they have this image of reliability because for so many years that was a core brand message.
- Rolls-Royce = quality. People will often refer to something that is outstanding as being the 'Rolls-Royce of...' This reputation was formed during the company's early years and still persists today. Its co-founder Henry Royce is quoted as saying: "Strive for perfection in everything you do. Take the best that exists and make it better. When it does not exist, design it."
- BMW = the ultimate driving machine. The company presents itself as the perfect connection between man and machine when it comes to road transport.

There are a lot of other cars out there that, despite millions being spent on advertising and branding over the years, have no clear and distinctive message. How often do we hear of 'Japanese' or 'American' cars being referred to in a generic sense? That is partly because, in this market at least, they have regularly changed their messages over the years or because they have never examined just what makes them different or unique.

Most cars these days are reliable, safe and go pretty fast if you want them to. In that sense, there is not much to distinguish one from another, so the branding for cars is important because it connects with people on an emotional level. It is not a logical thing, but an emotional one. Such a branding message used time and time again will get the ideas across.

On a much smaller scale, there is a recruitment company in Market Harborough called Vanilla. The name Vanilla was chosen partly to help with the branding. The company is able to use imagery to do with sweets in its branding to create the idea of nice, colourful things. It uses pleasant images in its marketing that extend by association to the company. It is a very different example of how the brand of a company can be used to create a distinctive and memorable message which can be used in its e-mails, on the website, in direct mail letters and so on – all at minimal cost.

Create a clear visual symbol

Do you have a strong visual symbol – normally called a logo – associated with your company? These can come from some fairly unusual areas - remember Tate and Lyle's decomposing lion? McDonalds has the world famous 'Golden Arches'; Nike has its 'swoosh'. With Coca-Cola, you have the bottle shape and the distinctive, red and the white lettering that is used. But the product itself, the bottle, is a very important part of the branding because it creates a symbol.

When you think about Dulux, you think about the old English sheepdog. Many is the time we have heard those dogs referred to as 'Dulux dogs'. I used to do some PR work for Hush Puppies. Here again, the breed of dog used in the Hush Puppies campaign – a basset hound – is often referred to as being the 'Hush Puppies' dog. You also have the golden Labrador 'Andrex puppy'.

The insurance service Direct Line originally used a bright red telephone when it launched its direct insurance service to the public. The concept was to cut out agents – the middlemen – so the public could buy insurance direct over the phone. Now Direct Line's phone logo has been joined by a bright red computer mouse because naturally its website now handles the majority of new enquiries.

Another classic visual symbol is the signature of the founder of the company. This tells the customer: "It's good enough for me to put my name to it." Kellogg's, Cadbury's and Disney all ensured that their surnames became linked with qualities that the public wanted.

These are all very different examples of different types of companies, but they all have a strong, clear visual symbol that people will look at and make an instant association: "Ah, it has to be Coke because look at the shape of the bottle", or "It has to be a Walt Disney film because of the signature at the beginning". It helps these companies stand out from the competition and is a way of helping people remember the product.

Clear position within the market

A good brand has a good idea about where it stands in the marketplace, whether it's at the top of the marketplace or the bottom. Lidl supermarket sells food, Harrods sells food. You can see they are both grocers, but most people wouldn't consider them to be in direct competition because they operate in different areas of the grocery retail sector.

The fact is that they sell the same commodity but you wouldn't ever get the two confused because they clearly position themselves for different audiences.

If you think of Harrods, you think of things that are very expensive and high quality. It used to be known as the place where 'Top people shop'. It has a certain image about it. Tourists visit Harrods when they come to London. This brand has become a destination on the tourist map just as much as Buckingham Palace.

People shop at Lidl for very different reasons. In their minds, it is a place that they can get cheap stuff. It is very competitively priced, it has some impressive pricing on everyday food items and this is the position Lidl has in the marketplace.

A fascinating example of market positioning is the quality clothing store Joules, head quartered in Market Harborough. This is an operation that knows exactly who its customers are and that in turn informs what it does in every part of its branding. Joules' branding is remarkably consistent. In its catalogue, every single photograph shows off the product in its best light, but it also enhances the brand image that Joules has created.

Imagine a time of endless golden summers from the 1950s –

that is part of the image that Joules captures with its styling and vision of 'Living the good life'. It has these endless idyllic summers with happy children and happy parents. This imagery plays across everything that Joules does. The posters it was using at the time were almost re-creations of the GWR or LNER railway posters of the 1940s and 1950s. But for all the nostalgia, it feels modern and contemporary – not an easy feat to pull off.

In my view – and judging by the success of the company – it has its branding absolutely spot on. They are very clear where they are. Price doesn't really come into it; when Joules sells wellies, people aren't thinking about how much they cost, but the design and look – things that a distinct group of people want to buy. They are buying into the whole Joules lifestyle.

Contrast this with another highly successful company, Ryan Air. Now Ryan Air has ingrained within it 'cheap flying'. Its chairman, Michael O'Leary, commented when launching a new route to Germany: "Jürgen [Weber, Lufthansa chairman] says Germans don't like low fares. How does he know? The Germans will crawl bollock-naked over broken glass to get them."

It's pretty clear what is at the centre of Ryan Air's branding message – we are the cheapest. Its advertising looks cheap even though some of the spots it takes out in the national press will be anything but. People would not necessarily associate the company with customer service (O'Leary is also quoted as telling a customer who questioned the no-refund policy: "What part of 'no refund' don't you understand? You are not getting a refund.")

Ryan Air's message appears to be purely about the price and being as cheap as possible. And at the time of writing, it is the fastest growing and most profitable airline in Europe so it would be reasonable to conclude that has found its position within the market.

When I worked at the advertising agency ABM in London, it had the Cusson's Imperial Leather account. Cusson's doesn't advertise much on television anymore, but for a long time through the 1970s and early '80s, it did advertise with the message 'Luxury you can afford every day'. This was a clear position for the market because Cusson's was saying was that it was luxury, top quality soap, but it was not so expensive that it couldn't be used every day.

So, where are you positioned in the market? Are you at the top, middle, bottom or are you an affordable luxury? You might be a distress purchase, in which case you are positioning yourself as being an essential purchase that people have to buy, whether they want to or not.

It is very important in terms of branding to decide where you are in the mind of your customer. What do they get when they buy your product?

Increase the value of the business

Is branding an exercise in navel gazing? Or could it, in the long term, be one of the ways to increase the value of your business? Let's look at some of the larger companies in the world. Nike, the American owned sportswear company, is known across the globe. Olympic athletes, top footballers and for that matter musicians are proud to wear the famous Nike 'swoosh' across their chests or on their shoes. With sales at the time of writing that have topped £30 billion, you would probably assume that Nike was one of the world's top brands. You would be wrong – in fact it is not even in the top 20.

Here is a list of top brands, compiled by *Businessweek* in 2007, ranked by estimated value in US dollars with percentage change on the previous year. Remember these figures are the value of the brand, not the company.

Coca-Cola (US)	$67 billion	-1%
Microsoft (US)	$56.9 billion	-5%
IBM (US)	$56.2 billion	+5%
General Electric (US)	$48.9 billion	+4%
Intel (US)	$32.3 billion	-9%
Nokia (Finland)	$30.1 billion	+14%
Toyota (Japan)	$27.9 billion	+12%
Disney (US)	$27.8 billion	+5%
McDonald's (US)	$27.5 billion	+6%
Mercedes (Germany)	$21.8 billion	+9%
Citi (US)	$21.5 billion	+7%
Marlboro (US)	$21.4 billion	+1%
Hewlett-Packard (US)	$20.5 billion	+8%
American Express (US)	$19.6 billion	+6%
BMW (Germany)	$19.6 billion	+15%
Gillette (US)	$19.6 billion	+12%
Louis Vuitton (France)	$17.6 billion	+10%
Cisco (US)	$17.5 billion	+6%
Honda (Japan)	$17.1 billion	+8%
Samsung (South Korea)	$16.2 billion	+8%

That was in 2007. Interestingly, for the first time in decades, in

2009 there has been a new No 1 in the branding chart. And it does not even feature in the top 20 of this survey from just two years previous. It's Google, a company that has its branding and logo seen in more than half the households in the UK every day.

So, how can you increase the value of your business through a brand? It's about being consistent, following the principles discussed in this section and not diluting the brand: be clear what it stands for, what the qualities behind it are, and stick with them. You create a valuable brand by going for the long-term vision. Anything about the brand has to be a consistent and in line with what your audience would expect from you. They buy a brand because they trust it to do what it has delivered in the past.

You can also learn from how the biggest players protect their brand. If Coca-Cola ever has any problems with bottling or distribution, it immediately gets fixed because the last thing that Coke wants is something that in some way insinuates its brand is inferior to other products. That would be completely unacceptable to the company that wants to get the most out of its brand. When Cadbury's had an issue with salmonella in one of its chocolate bars in June 2006, it automatically recalled more than one million bars. Customers trust Cadbury's and that trust is essential to its reputation for quality.

Use your brand to launch new products

Increasingly, large companies are not releasing new products, but instead launch something that extends the value of an existing brand. Take Pepsi-Cola. When Pepsi decided to launch a low calorie version of its product, it launched Diet Pepsi. More recently, because Diet Pepsi is aimed at women, the company launched Pepsi Max. It is a very similar drink, slightly stronger in taste, but is aimed at men who like to 'Take it to the Max'. Pepsi is using the success of its brand to launch umbrella products.

Another good example of this is Mars. Mars is well known for its chocolate and confectionery brands, including Mars bars, Milky Way and Snickers. In the 1980s, it began a campaign of brand extensions, some of which worked and some of which were less successful. Mars ice creams and milk shakes used the popular chocolate bar but transferred them into different areas. The ice cream in particular meant sales in the hot summer months were maintained as consumers switched from chocolate bars to ice cream bars.

This extension of a well-known brand has led to other companies following a similar route. Mars created greater brand awareness and has encouraged people to buy Mars all year round. By lending the credibility of the Mars brand to the ice cream sector, the company tapped into impulse buying sales. Mars did a lot of research to that end in blind taste tests and consumer surveys and found that people were more interested and more likely to buy a Mars ice cream than a similar bar ice cream with a different name.

Mars is a famous international company, but brand extensions work for many different sized companies and sectors. Voice Connect is a telecoms company based near Groby in Leicestershire. It started using the letters 'VC' in front of all its products. Within the telecoms industry, it is quite well known that all Voice Connect's products start with VC. This simple branding means that it was much easier to start naming products. It has developed a range of products that all begin with VC as a way of making it clear to people in a range of markets that this is a Voice Connect product.

This simple branding device within a business-to-business context is a way of launching new products but under the umbrella of an existing brand. If you've been working hard to get well known, and people know who you are within your particular sector and if you've been thinking of launching a new product and your company is going to be a good quality reflection of the main company, it is a great idea to use this umbrella brand.

Highlights a clear benefit for the consumer

I mentioned earlier the logo used by Direct Line. When Direct Line insurance first launched 20 years ago, it was a car insurance company. It was a way of cutting out the middlemen, the agents who arranged car insurance. The savings on their commission were passed on to the customer. It was a radical idea at the time – to pick up the phone, speak to somebody on the line, and renew your insurance quote... no other company at the time could do that.

Obviously, other companies copied the idea, but Direct Line continued to innovate and is now using the Internet heavily. In its early stages, its message was all about this clear benefit for the customers. How did the company position that in the mind of the consumer? It used a very simple image of a phone that was shaped like a car on wheels. It came on the TV screen and rang a few musical notes at the end of every advert. Later on, once the online service started, Direct Line used a similar device with a red computer mouse. Those two visual images are still being used.

As small business owners, we are in danger of being too close to the product or to the service that we offer. We say: '"It's a bit dull, people are used to that and they know what to expect, maybe it is time to change it and scrap it, move on to something completely different."

Perhaps these were the thoughts that were running through the heads of Royal Mail bosses when they decided that the name no longer reflected its new thrusting corporate image. Surely the public would prefer a new modern name and image? So Consignia was born in January 2001 and proved so popular that after spending more than £2 million on the exercise, the company decided to scrap it within 13 months.

I'm not saying that you shouldn't ever reconsider your branding, but often it is a question of updating or refining what you already have rather than ditching it all and starting again.

So be very careful about making any sweeping changes without thinking them through. Once you change, you should stay with the message for a long time. Remember how Kellogg's Frosties has stuck with Tony the Tiger. He has changed over the six decades plus that he has advertised Frosties, but essentially he is still the same character and has added millions to the value of the brand.

Pre-Launch Checklist - Branding

☐ Be clear about your product, what it stands for in everything you do. At its simplest level, think about your logo and general image. If you have bright red in your logo, make sure that everything you've got has that same shape/pattern.

☐ A clear and simple message is always best. Don't overcomplicate. Know where you are going and aim for a clear, simple, straightforward message to your customer base.

☐ Think about your target audience. If you are aiming your product mainly at women, that will have an influence on the language, colours and shapes that you might want to use. If you are aiming your product mainly at senior managers, that will have an impact on the imagery and colours you use. Most things in marketing start from the knowledge of who your target market is. Be clear about the people or sector you are aiming at as the foundation for your brand proposition.

☐ Why are you different? What is it that sets you apart from other companies? If there is something of value that is even a little different, that is something to focus on and maximise in your message. Burger King sells hamburgers, as do most of its competitors. Burger King focuses on its 'flame grilled' whoppers. That is something its main competitors don't have.

Time to change? When you have spent a lot of time thinking about something and have got it right, don't be in a rush to change. Don't start changing your branding just for the sake of it, because you're bored with it. The chances are you will be bored with it long before your customers have even started to remember the message.

Chapter 2

Advertising your products or services

• Where to advertise • Gaining attention •
Negotiating a discount • 'Reason why' advertising •
Testing strategies • Advertising at its best •

> Advertising – a powerful way to communicate an idea quickly
> to the market.

Many people confuse marketing with advertising. Advertising
is one part of a marketing strategy. Advertising is
promotional material that is paid for and that can appear in many
different media, including newspapers, magazines, TV, radio, the
Internet and posters. This chapter is mainly about press advertising.
However, many of these principles can be transferred over to any
area of advertising media, should you wish to use them.

It is important to note at the outset that the majority of
advertising does not work – that is, it does not make money for
the company which paid for its creation. It loses money, by any

definition or measurement that you care to use. What's perhaps worse, most people who advertise do not actually know whether their advertising works. They advertise in various places, enquiries come in and they assume that it is a mix of the adverts that work.

If you take nothing else away from this section, remember this: you want your advertising to be profitable. There is no reason why any advert you produce cannot bring you back double, triple or even 10 times the cost of running it.

These ideas will give you the tools to do this. You will almost certainly find that the first time you run an advert using these ideas it will work better than your old adverts, and that the longer you persist and test out slightly different ideas, the more effective it will be. The aim is to have an advert that you are confident will work every time you run it; an advert like this is a huge business asset.

Where to advertise

If you stick a poster in the middle of a deserted field in the Highlands, it's pretty obvious that nobody is going to see it and the only interest will be from the odd passing cow. So before you think about how to advertise your business, you need to think about the potential audience that you want to attract and identify the best way to reach that audience.

Some factors you should take into account are:

- Where do my prospects live?
- Are they willing to travel?
- If they are willing to travel, how far will they come?

- How much money do they have to spend?
- If I am solving a problem, how do they currently solve that problem?
- Is there a better way of getting to them than advertising?
- Which publications do they read?
- Is there a section of the publication that is most popular?
- What other companies advertise in this publication?
- Does it work for them? (Ask them.)

Sometimes you don't have much choice in which publication you use to advertise. You might have only one trade publication or one key local newspaper. This has its advantages and disadvantages. On the down side, this will limit the amount of discount you will receive. On the plus side, it prevents fragmentation of your audience and probably means that this one title is well read.

Who will see my advert?

Always ask for proof of circulation. Don't believe what people tell you over the phone. It's easy to make up the number of readers and advertising sales people are often prone to stretching the truth. If possible, advertise in titles that have ABC audited circulation. It is also important to find out the types of job and seniority of the people who read the title.

Readership: Many titles will claim that each copy is read by two or three people in addition to the buyer or subscriber. This may be possible, but in my experience rarely is. For every copy of a magazine that is read by two people, there is a copy that lies unread – or worse, is never delivered.

Longevity of publication: It makes sense to advertise in titles that have a longer shelf life. A monthly title stays around for weeks, if not months. People hang onto these types of titles because they think they will refer back to them. Daily titles tend to be well read but quickly disposed of. This means that if you have a sale this weekend, they can work well. But a more general advert is less likely to work.

Respect for title: We all have a tendency to dismiss the trade magazine we know. Because we know the subject well, we can see through the stuff and nonsense that can dominate such titles. However, most sectors have at least one title that is more respected than the others. It is the 'authority' title in the industry. As a general rule, these are the best titles to advertise in because the serious players will read this title.

Disposable income of readership: It is one thing to be in a title that has 20,000 'readers', but another to be in a title with 20,000 'buyers'. How many of the readers could buy what you are offering? And out of those, how many have the disposable income or the authority to spend their company's money to buy what you are offering? Having the intention is great – but having the cash is better.

How many are interested in what you are selling?

The final key point to take into account is that out of all these people, how many in reality could actually buy what you are selling? You may find it is a tiny percentage of the total number. This doesn't mean it isn't worth advertising – but it can be worth taking into account and is certainly a good tool to use when negotiating a discount.

The cost of the advert: How much the advert costs is, in a way, unimportant. This is because it is relative to how much money the advert brings in. So an advert that costs £200 is expensive if it brings in only £100 in sales. However, an advert that costs £2,000 is cheap if it brings in £10,000 in sales. Often, the only way to know just how much cash an advert brings in is when you know the average lifetime value of a customer.

'Lifetime value': A customer may reply to an advert and spend £10. However, the real aim of the advert should be to create a new customer which means that over time they keep coming back to you for more and perhaps one day may spend £10,000. Work out how much your average customer is worth to give you a better idea of how much value an enquiry will really give you.

'Off the page advertising' or ways of generating leads

What do you want your advert to do? Is it to sell 'off the page' or is it to generate leads? Be clear what the central aim of your advert is and make your advert work to that goal.

Price per enquiry: You probably have some idea how many people you will need to have enquire before you make a sale. For some industries it is one in 10 – for others it might be almost one in one. Your price per enquiry is the number of enquiries you receive for every pound you spend on advertising. So a £500 advert that produces 10 enquiries means that each lead costs you

£50. How profitable the advert is depends entirely on how much your service costs and how many of those 10 you are able to convert.

Negotiating the rate card

The rate card of most magazines is a work of fiction. It is no more than a starting point for negotiations. Treat is as such. The people who sell advertising space will expect you to negotiate a discount. The minimum discount is 15 per cent. Magazines discount 15 per cent when they sell to advertising agencies (their cut) for booking the space. You should get at least this. You can get varying amounts depending on other circumstances including:

- The dominance of the title within the sector.
- How long the title has been going.
- The reputation of the title.
- Profile of readers – how many really fit your profile?
- Demand for space. Does the title regularly advertise other magazines in its publishing stable? Do you see multiple adverts for their own reader services? This means that they have been unable to sell all the advertising space and are therefore keen to sell space in the future.
- Proximity to deadline. Nothing focuses the mind of an advertising sales person more than a looming deadline. Discounts of up to 90 per cent have been given close to the publication date for those willing to play brinkmanship.

The advert itself

What are you hoping to achieve from running this advert? What do you want people to take away from it? Are you looking to build general awareness of your company or your brand? This general approach to branding or 'just getting your message out there' is a very expensive, very long-term growth strategy, and I wouldn't normally recommend it. You want each advert to deliver specific enquiries that can be measured.

Is your advert a one-off or part of a series? Are you looking for a quick hit or to build a relationship with readers? In the latter case, you will benefit from a recognisable identity. I would suggest that it makes sense to create a house style for your advertising campaigns as suggested in Chapter 1.

The headline: Your headline is one of five key factors that will influence the success of your advert. It should be benefit led and make it clear why people should read on.

A successful headline will stop the correct reader. This means that you are happy for non-qualified people to pass you by. If you are selling to FDs then it's okay if marketing directors pass you by. You're not selling to them. This means that the function of the advert is to exclude as well as entice.

Here are some successful headlines and the subheads that amplify the message:

The credit crunch is over

Low rate finance available today for manufacturing companies looking to expand in 2010

Evil, wicked temptation from your newsagent
Blackfriars Flapjacks – available at all good newsagents

Laughter isn't the best medicine
Benylin – when you're serious about feeling better

These headlines will stop a proportion of their target audience when combined with a suitable image and persuasive copy.

'Reason why advertising'

The term 'reason why advertising' was coined at the turn of the previous century. It is probably the single most important advance in marketing. It has often been copied but never bettered. It was developed by John E Kennedy (no relation to John F Kennedy) and is the basis for all good advertising.

You can download an e-book of *Scientific Advertising,* the book in which he reveals the ideas behind reason why advertising from, *www.themarketingmentor.co.uk*

Its simple theory is that we all need a reason why to buy. The colour, cost and company name may all have an influence on us, but essentially we need a clear benefit TO US – 'what's in it for me?' Make the benefit clear enough and people will buy. Clever words aren't enough as people can see what you are trying to do. Clever words might impress your friends, but will not in themselves sell.

Worry less about clever puns and more about simple benefits. Instead of fluff and generalities, give your readers substance and facts that appeal to their self-interest.

Body copy: Once you are clear who you are writing to, where it is being read, what benefit the advert is about and what your headline is, the body copy of your advert will flow easily. Make your text clear and easy to read. Tell the reader what they need to know in order to make a decision. Use short and punchy sentences that a 12 year old can read and understand. Follow through from your headline and always end with a clear reason for the reader to act.

Contact details: Offer a choice of ways for potential clients to reach you. Some people (they tend to be the more proactive ones) prefer to make a phone call, but some people like to e-mail, fax or even text in their questions. You want to give them the choice. You also want to be as clear as possible which adverts are working for you so it's a good idea to either include a simple enquiry code linked to each advert or give the name of the person that they can ask for. That way, if people ask to talk to 'Harry' you know it is in response to the August issue of *What Hat?* magazine.

It then becomes your job to track reply rates to each advert. How many enquiries came in? How many of those converted into actual sales? Assuming each of those will spend the same as your customer average over time, you will quickly get an idea of which adverts have actually made (or lost) money and if so, how much.

Different styles of adverts

These are some of the main types of advert and the reason they tend to run.

Direct response – adverts that have the clear intention of asking the reader to do something, such as call a number and book/enquire. This direct approach is also the easiest way to tell whether an advert or publication is working.

Trade – this advert is not for the public, but for people likely to stock the products that can be sold to the trade. It can be very important if you want to explain to a retailer the benefits of selling on your product or service.

Corporate – a flag-waving advert that tells the world what a wonderful company you are. It's my least favourite type of advertising. However, it has its place when a company is being tuned for sale or in response to bad PR.

Brand building – this can be effective but is notoriously difficult to measure and the results are known only over long periods of time. Often the best approach for satisfying this need is to take out sponsorship in relevant publications that fit your customer profile.

Sponsorship – not strictly advertising, but as outlined above, it can be useful to build awareness of your business. It helps to make you known to your customers if you use the right types of publication. If you think your customers tune in to a local radio station for the weather or read a particular section of a newspaper, consider sponsoring it as a cost effective long term alternative to advertising.

Launch – there is a big difference between continual advertising and the initial launch campaign. Advertising can be very effective when something is brand new, so it makes sense to spend more money than normal in an intensive burst during the early days.

Advertising can certainly be effective, and works particularly well in certain situations; for example, when you have:

- a very clearly defined audience (such as housewives, bank managers or milkmen to pick three random examples).
- an upcoming event such as a music festival or an opening.
- a long-term image to build up. Car advertising and luxury goods favour this type of advertising because they often don't sell their product overnight. They need to slowly build up audience identification with the brand.
- something new to tell, such as a price reduction or a store opening.

Some other useful ideas to bear in mind when considering advertising:

Test the headline: If you can, test a version of the headline you are planning on using in the advert in a direct mail letter. If you have an appeal or offer that works as direct mail, it stands a good chance that it will also work in advert form. You can also try this approach with an e-mail marketing campaign.

Spend time getting the layout right: Experiment with different approaches, but don't try and get too clever. The best format for advertising was devised and tested by David Ogilvy in the 1960s and still works today. It is roughly one-third picture, one-third headline and one-third body copy. This ratio should be followed under normal circumstances, but if limited space means something needs to go, it is the picture that should go first.

Target key publications: Go for the top one or two titles in your market. Don't waste time on publications with a tiny circulation. They may be cheap, but they are cheap for a reason.

Google adwords: This is a big area in itself, and we cover it in depth in the Marketing Mentor session on the Internet, but this area is becoming increasingly important. It's a very clever way to target people and measure response.

Substance over silliness: We all laughed at funny lager TV commercials in the 1980s but did they really sell the product? You are better off creating campaigns that give people a reason to buy your product rather than have a giggle.

Consider 'advertorials': People buy magazines to read articles so it makes sense to at least consider giving them lots of interesting and relevant information – the same amount they would get in an article. This hybrid is usually paid for like an advert but designed to look like an article in the magazine. It will normally attract a higher readership if it's done properly.

Pre Launch Checklist – Advertising

☐ Consider what you want to achieve. Be clear in your objectives and what you want your advert to do – whether it is to create direct sales or fresh enquiries.

☐ Research the available publications. Buy the magazines and get a sense of what you like and don't like about them. Talk to other advertisers and look at the titles from your prospects' point of view.

☐ Negotiate a discount. Never pay full rate card – ever. You should always get 15 per cent off – you could get as much as 90 per cent off, depending on the deadlines and enthusiasm of the sales person.

☐ Test carefully. There is no point in advertising for the sake of it. Every advert should be there to bring you more money than it costs – even if that is over the long term.

☐ Think long term. Don't always expect to make money overnight. In the long term – sometimes known as the 'back end' – you will find far more profit than in a quick one-off sale.

Chapter 3

Brochures and leaflets that get noticed

- *First impressions count* • *Speak their language*
- *Solve their problem* • *Be specific* • *Alternatives to brochures* •

> An effective way to leave a tangible summary of the benefits your company offers to prospects.

If you are thinking about producing promotional material, you should insist that your next brochure or leaflet stops prospects in their tracks, keeps their attention and makes them want to find out more about you. It's all about creating a good first impression and a lasting memory of how you can help your prospects.

This chapter is about how to gain your prospects' attention and the specific techniques you can use to improve your customers' understanding of what you do, and therefore the likelihood that they will buy from you. In fact, if you implement all of the ideas here, you should be able to improve the impact of your brochure many times over. The ideas are proven and needn't cost you any more to produce than your present brochure.

Before you start

Everybody has some form of brochure or leaflet, but most of the examples I see are ineffective because they don't explain how that company can help its prospect. If your brochure spells out clearly what benefits you can offer your customer and nothing else, it will probably stand head and shoulders above those of your competitors.

Think about why you are creating your brochure in the first place. It is not to boast, or show off your new offices: it is purely a selling aid. Any pictures, text or diagrams are only there to explain how you can help your prospect in order to assist the selling process. Anything else has no place in a brochure.

Consider who you are creating your brochure for. Many companies still produce a 'one size fits all' brochure for existing clients and prospects from all industries. Before you fall into that trap too, ask yourself if all your customers buy for the same reasons, or if you have a different appeal for a number of different markets? Chances are you'll answer 'yes' to both those questions.

That should help you decide to make your brochure a carefully targeted, skilful piece of communication. What you don't want is to end up with a flabby, meaningless document that doesn't successfully talk to anybody. Sure, it may be glossy, but so is the finish on the outside of the waste paper basket – and that's where it's likely to end up.

If you do have a number of different markets that you are

aiming at, you should create a separate (but perhaps similar) brochure for each one. For example, let's assume that you have three main markets: one for butchers, one for bakers and one for candlestick makers. The product that you provide for each is fairly similar, but because you are a smart company, you have targeted these three niche areas. Your brochures spell out the distinct benefits that you can offer each market.

Don't let your specialist knowledge go to waste. If you understand your prospects' problems, why not tell them in language and imagery that they understand? Why let all your specialist knowledge go to waste when producing your brochure? By all means, decide on a common layout and theme for the three brochures, but select pictures for the cover that best reflect each market. Write at least the key sections of your text addressing the specific needs of the butcher, baker and candlestick maker.

Creating a series of specialist brochures will not be much more expensive to produce, but the end product will be many times more effective as a selling tool.

Make your brochure or leaflet direct response, not institutional. At every stage of your brochure, you want to make it easy for your prospect to contact you. It should contain a number of calls to action: at least one on each page.

Many brochures appear to be created to please the directors of a company rather than the customers. Remember, the only reason you want somebody to read about you in a brochure is so they will buy from you. The buying process may well occur in two or more stages, but you want the brochure that the prospect is reading to stir them into taking action. You want them to say: "I want to find out more about this product."

First impressions count

Remember that your cover is the first thing a prospect will see – therefore it should always contain a powerful headline and strong attention-generating image.

How important is the front page of your brochure? Ask any magazine editor if the front page of their magazine is important. More time is spent on the look and feel of the front page of a magazine than on any of the articles inside. They're competing for buyers, just like you are, and getting the right picture on the front can make a huge difference to the circulation in any given month. So take a leaf from their book: if you are using a picture, spend time selecting an interesting one.

People love looking at faces. The human brain is very good at seeing and remembering other people's faces and is amazingly sophisticated at it. One of the reasons that so many magazine covers have close-cropped photographs of faces is that such an image is almost impossible for us to ignore. In tests of magazine covers, the close-cropped photographs of faces are looked at more quickly and remembered far better than any other image. Although this treatment may not be exactly right for your brochure, you should at least consider using a face somewhere on its cover.

If you are using colour, the front page is certainly the place to use it. In fact, even if your brochure is largely in black and white, it is often worth the expense of using at least two colours on the front and back to achieve maximum impact.

For general use, select bright and light colours with plenty of space. A dark cover with crowded text implies a dense, difficult read and will put people off even opening your brochure.

Certain colour combinations work well together to attract the human eye. For example, red and yellow force us to look. When orange and purple are used together, the orange appears incredibly bright and attractive – ask any fruit and vegetable stall holder.

Speak their language

When you are writing a brochure, don't just think about what your products are; consider the problems that your customers may be currently facing. In fact, don't just think about this, ask your customers what problems they are facing. For example, you may assume that your customers are most concerned about price, when in fact the biggest concern is speed of delivery. If they can have delivery of any item that you have in stock within 24 hours, they will happily pay more because they can pass the extra charge on to their clients.

If you know what the main concern of your client is, that should be the core focus of your brochure. Now, if you also happen to be competitive on price and offer a wider range of services, so much the better.

But remember that these are extras. You must address their main concerns first, so if it's speed they're after, the whole body of the brochure needs to focus on this. The cover could show a blurred member of staff running towards the reader. The colours could be red and yellow. Subheadings could include words like 'rocket' or 'rush' or 'instant'. The whole style of the document should reflect that specific concern of your core customer.

Keep your copy informative, but factual. As a general rule, people do not enjoy being 'sold to'. They usually have a problem that requires solving, and if your product or service meets their needs, then they are more than happy to hear about it. However, clients are not overly keen on the selling part.

If you think about it, people buy a newspaper to read the news, not the advertisements. So, if you can, make the copy in your brochure as impartial, factual and interesting to read as possible. That should make your readership soar. The message that you want to get across will be digested, believed and acted upon.

Write copy that is interesting to the reader. Obviously this is a whole area in itself, but there are some quick guidelines:

- Keep sentences short. Shorter sentences are easier to read. Reduce the size of paragraphs; blocks of too much text appear daunting to the reader. Use subheadings between paragraphs.
- Use the word 'you' far more often than 'I' or 'we'. People are much more interested in themselves and their problems than your company.
- Don't use excessive industry or technical jargon. It's not going to impress anybody and it won't sell your product.
- Try to follow a logical structure in your argument: Do you have this problem? Have you tried this, but found that it didn't work? You may also have had this experience. Here's what you can do about it today.

Before you pass your material on to be printed, try to get as many people to proof read it as possible. Not just for punctuation, but to see whether your ideas have come through and make sense to different types of readers from outside your company. You may have overlooked some very simple points that will put the whole of your brochure in context.

Typefaces: keep them simple and easy to read. On your PC you will have several hundred typefaces. Just because they are there does not mean that you need to use them. We have all had fun experimenting with typefaces in posters or letters but a brochure is not the place to do this. As a general rule for most brochures, you need only two typefaces.

For the body copy, Times, Times New Roman or Garamond are good choices. They are serif typefaces – they have little feet on the vertical strokes – and as such are easy typefaces for the eye to read and remember. Studies show that our understanding is nine times better when these typefaces are used; we can also read four times as quickly.

If you don't believe me, try this simple test. Next time somebody has sent you an e-mail that you are struggling to understand, convert it into Garamond. Instantly it will appear clearer and you will be able to read it far faster. You will also understand sentences that before you found incomprehensible.

For headlines and subheads, use a different typeface such as Arial or Gills Sans. These are examples of sans serif typefaces – no feet on the vertical strokes. These typefaces work well for the short subheads that break up paragraphs, headlines at the start of a section or for contact phone numbers at the bottom of your page. They also create variety and add a change of visual pace to your document. These are both important factors in encouraging your reader to keep on reading.

Solve their problems

Give your customers a convincing reason for buying from you. In your brochure, ask yourself with every paragraph: "Is this giving my customer a real inducement to buy their services from me?" Explain why your flour offers the baker excellent value for money and tell them why your reliable delivery service means that they won't have angry suppliers wondering where their bread is.

Give your prospects enough compelling reasons why they should use your service so that using anybody else would appear foolish. Don't forget the basics. It can be easy to get caught up in the detail, but remember to explain in simple terms what your company actually does!

Be specific: When most people think of a brochure, they think of a big fat corporate document that sales people leave behind, or a piece of junk mail that is posted out. Few companies produce a brochure that is actually of any real interest to their prospects. One of the reasons for this is that traditionally, because of the expense associated with producing brochures, they had to be a 'one size fits all' and communicate with too broad a market.

If your company works in different sectors, then it is far better to create a series of shorter, punchy brochures aimed at each of these markets, than one grand brochure aimed at nobody in particular.

You may even have one product that essentially remains the same, but by creating different campaigns – and therefore brochures – it can be aimed at different markets.

Examples of different markets where it would be appropriate:

- Sports shoes – brochures aimed at the serious runner and the fashion market.
- Hotels – brochures aimed at the weekend holiday maker, the business traveller and the conference organiser.
- Marketing company – brochures aimed at start-up companies and mature businesses.
- Telecoms company specialising in health sector – brochures aimed at GPs, NHS Trusts and PCTs.

Style and substance

Caption everything. A photograph without a caption is a puzzle to the reader. You may know that it is a photograph of your managing director, or a group of staff from your call centre, but the reader will not have a clue.

If possible, include a benefit within the caption as well. For example, a caption for call centre staff could be: "Over 200 staff are employed in our Market Harborough call centre ensuring that customer enquiries can be swiftly answered 24 hours a day." A caption of the MD could read: "Fred Bloggs has been the managing director of Best Bakers for the past 12 years, and has been personally responsible for the customer care initiatives that have proved so popular with clients."

Any promotional material should be professionally printed.

The first impression many people will have of your company is from your brochure. You may have put a great deal of thought into its content, but if it is obviously printed on a home printer, this creates a very poor first impression.

This does not mean that you need to produce a full-colour extravaganza on thick matt paper. Far from it. Often a simpler approach will work better with your target market. In fact, if you are following an earlier point and are considering producing several more targeted brochures, the slight extra cost in this can be offset by printing a more thoughtful two-colour brochure, rather than always going for the expensive option. If your printer always advises that full colour is best, beware. It may be best for their profits, but not always for you.

Work out what style is most appropriate for your customer. If you are selling a luxury product costing thousands of pounds, you cannot expect a photocopied A4 leaflet to sell your product for you. Similarly, if you are selling into a price sensitive market, overtly expensive brochures may make a potential customer question your profit margins.

Perception is your customers' reality; so much of how your company's image is created comes from the quality of your brochure. With the possible exception of a few fine jewellers or purveyors other luxury products, snobbery does not work well. You need to position yourself as being on a similar level to the potential customer. This should be reflected in the style of writing, layout and printing. There is no right or wrong, only the most appropriate. Fancy designs in themselves are neither good nor bad; it all depends on the target market you wish to reach.

One area where you should not skimp is photography. Use

high quality photographs or illustrations throughout. If you are going to use a photograph, use it for a reason. If it is there for a reason, then it must communicate with the reader. If it reproduces poorly or was badly taken in the first place, it is probably best to either re-take it, or leave it out. An unclear image detracts from your message, your organisation's stature and weakens your credibility.

If you are going to use a cartoon to illustrate the point that you wish to make, only use clip art as a very last resort. Too many people will know what it is and this will lessen the impact of your material. If you can possibly afford to, it is best to commission an illustrator to create a punchy cartoon that makes your point. A simple black and white cartoon costs as little as £50: a small price to pay in order to make the point you are aiming for.

Bonus material

Here are some examples of offers and incentives that you can include within your brochure to increase and measure response:

- Include a free sample of your product with the brochure.
- Print on the back a money-off coupon to be claimed. This is a great way of determining if your brochure has been effective.
- Include a limited offer with your brochure and manually time stamp in a specific date by which the offer must be claimed.
- Give away a bundle of free extras if they order today.

This could ideally include valuable information which is cheap for you to produce, but important to your customer.

- Include free vouchers if they order before a certain date. These could be vouchers such as £5 off if you spend £50 in one transaction, or a percentage discount off the total price.

- Offer a free two-hour consultation. This will appeal to any serious prospect because it puts the onus on you to prove that you can deliver what you promise.

- A '2 for the price of 1' offer can work well if you want to increase the likelihood of somebody trying out your product or service for the first time.

- Some prospects are apprehensive that if they call, you will try to sell them something. A less threatening alternative is to offer them a recorded message which explains what you offer. Some people will prefer to hear about what you do rather than read about it.

- You can offer a password to a limited access website area. This makes them feel unique and trusted, and can lead to other special offers and limited availability items.

- Including a special bonus to claim if they act within seven days is a popular offer in direct mail letters – but why not include it within your brochure or leaflet to make a response more urgent?

- A free report on their sector can also speed up response – especially if it contains advice that will specifically help your ideal prospect. There is more about this in the 'Alternatives to brochures' section.

All of these and more will give your prospect a strong reason to take action and find out more about your company. In your brochure you need to give them a very real and direct incentive for picking up the phone now (rather than later) and finding out more about your bonus, report, offer etc.

Leaflets and flyers

Flyers are essentially mini brochures that follow most of the same rules. The main difference is how much information you can put across. Flyers work best when they focus on one key benefit, area or theme.

Disposable. One of the great things about flyers is that they can be very disposable. You can create a flyer for an event, a launch, a season and not worry that it will become quickly out of date. From Christmas to Halloween to January sales, flyers can be powerful topical mini brochures giving your customers reasons to visit or buy.

Don't try to be too clever. People have a very short attention span when it comes to flyers. So don't go into too much detail and try to explain everything you do. Stick to one or two bold ideas that can be expressed quickly rather than laying out your complete list of services.

Because of the nature of the flyer, it also allows you to be topical and time sensitive so you can incorporate current offers and promotions.

Alternatives to brochures

The main aims of a brochure are usually to establish your expertise in what you do, ensure that your phone number and contact details are accessible for the prospect and to give your business a kind of physical presence – acting as a reminder in their office.

If this is what you want your brochure to do, an alternative to brochures may work as well or even better for you. There are three main alternatives, and depending on what you do and what message you want to get across, all three may be useful.

Tips booklets: These are the quickest and easiest to produce and give you a kind of instant expertise. The easiest way to create them is to decide on a topic that is of interest to your customers that you can help with. So for example, The Ideal Marketing Company came up with a booklet of ideas on how business owners can cope with the economic downturn through better marketing.

Once you have decided on a topic, get a group of staff together and give yourselves five minutes to come up with as many tips as you can on that topic. Everybody just writes them down, without editing or checking what other people have put. Then one person collects these and writes them up as tips, expanding on them, re-writing as necessary etc. The end result is a selection of between 10 to 50 tips or snippets of advice that your potential customers would find helpful.

Special reports: This is an opportunity for you to carry out some research into a problem facing your customers and then work out how you can help them. Find an area of concern, research the background to it, what opportunities there are in the area and what the solutions are – presumably you are linked to one or more of these solutions. A special report is usually between five and 10 pages long and can include graphs, photos and illustrations where appropriate.

Audio visual: A third alternative is to leave paper behind altogether and look at either a CD or DVD. A CD can comprise anything from an interview with the MD, a script about what the company does, interviews with satisfied customers or a recording of a talk. If your customers are likely to be driving to and from their office in the morning, they can listen to your audio in the car on the way there or while at their PC.

If you have a bit more money to spend, especially if your product is a suitable subject, then a video can be very effective. Corporate videos can be used on websites, burned onto disk or used as part of a sales person's demo. The right combination of pictures and music can connect with emotions far better than the written word. So, if you want to touch or inspire people, video may be the best way to do it. But be warned: choose your video production company with care as there are many companies out there who can make your product look cheap and tacky. Make sure you like the work they produce before committing to anything.

The nine pitfalls

I've given you several areas to think about to help you create a brochure that will increase your response rates significantly. Each component will increase either your readership or their comprehension. As a result, your response levels should rise significantly, unless you are selling to the wrong market or you have a product or service that nobody wants to buy. However, under normal circumstances, if you combine these various elements, the number of people enquiring should go through the roof.

But beware. There are a number of pitfalls that can wreck your response levels. Heed these warnings and make sure that your brochure avoids these failings.

1. Doesn't explain what you can offer the customer. It's easy to get caught up in the details and forget the bigger picture. The best brochure should lead the reader to a logical conclusion. That might be a special offer or free sample. But nobody will think of buying anything from you if it is not clear what you have on offer. So make sure you explain clearly in your brochure what you do, why you do it and why this is helpful for the prospect. You'll be surprised how often people leave this out!

2. Creates the wrong image for your business. When you put together any form of communication, you should ask yourself what sort of impression you want to leave the reader with. Begin with this in mind. You might decide that you want the image of a hand-crafted cottage industry that has been

unchanged by time, using traditional ingredients and recipes. If that's the case, then everything about your brochure, from the text to the layout, needs to reflect this. Don't mention that you were only founded in 2002 and don't show your fleet of delivery motorbikes on the front page.

3. Out of date style or content. Changing material for the sake of it is usually a mistake, but it is important to keep your style fresh. Kellogg's regularly change elements of their logo or characters, but the Honey Monster and Tony the Tiger are still there in a contemporary way. Watch out for unfashionable clothes, large mobile telephones and outdated hairstyles in photographs of people. Few things date faster. Also, it makes sense to involve a designer, or rely on the experience of a printer to offer you advice on what will work best.

4. So general that it says nothing. Everybody claims that they offer great service at an affordable price. It is a phrase that means almost nothing because of its overuse. Don't be bland. If you are going to make a claim, make it specific. Offer the best service in Luton or your money back. Offer 48-hour delivery on all items not in stock – guaranteed. Tell customers specific facts that are of interest to them and that give them a reason to buy from you, rather than a competitor.

5. Bland writing and design that is difficult to read. Some designers get carried away with producing a work of art that is almost impossible to read. It might look great, but it will bring you no business. However, if you have no design in your brochure, and it is just large blocks of text, your

readership will also drop. You need to work with a designer who understands that the purpose of design is to enhance the text and the message that it contains. Clarity is important and if the reader struggles to read your message, then you have no hope of persuading them to your point of view.

6. A variety of typeface styles that is confusing and hard to read. In almost all cases, two typefaces are all you need: a serif typeface for the body copy and a sans serif typeface for the subheads and headlines. That's it. If you overload your reader with all manner of fonts, you will confuse, bewilder and lose their interest. Keep your fonts clear and easy to read with good spacing and you will greatly increase the likelihood of prospects reading your text.

7. No way to get in touch with you. Some people will not want to phone you, they would rather e-mail or fax you. Give them the choice and make it as easy as possible for them to get in touch. Give them your details on every page and have a page or a section towards the back of your brochure where they have clear instructions as to how they can take the next step.

8. It's boring! While you may have been paid to create your brochure, nobody is paid to read it. So if it's boring and irrelevant, they will stop and throw it away. Cut out unnecessarily flowery language, minimise jargon and make it interesting to the reader.

   The best way to make it interesting is to make it relevant. If somebody wants to know how to make more money, tell them what you can do to help them make more money! If somebody wants to improve the safety of their staff, show them how you will protect them. Don't be coy – spell out your advantages in a relevant, straightforward way and make it interesting. The motto of one well-known advertising agency from the 1920s was 'The truth well told.' The truth is always interesting if you tell it in a way that is relevant to your target audience.

9. There is no incentive to buy. After they have read your material, you don't want people thinking, "that was quite interesting, I'll bear it in mind for some possible future occasion." You want to guide them into taking action by giving them easy-to-follow steps to reach you. You may want to give them options of what to do now, or spell out the details of your time-sensitive offer. Whatever you do, it is important they realise that if they don't do something now, they may forget about what they have just learned. They should put the wheels in motion immediately, otherwise they'll lose out in the future.

Other ideas and suggestions

Risk reversal: The power of risk reversal will help you sell to a stranger. The hardest sale that you will ever make is to a person who doesn't know about your good reputation. In your brochure you are attempting to say to this stranger: "Look, we have a good understanding of what your problems are, we know that you have found your current supplier a problem in the past, here is why we feel that we are different." If you are confident that your product or service is good, risk reversal is a very powerful way to dramatically increase the number of strangers willing to try your wares. At the very least, I'd urge you to experiment with this strategy, and a brochure is a good place to do this.

Risk reversal No 1: Tell your prospect: "We feel you will be delighted with the quality of your candlesticks, the reliability of our delivery and the price that we offer. We don't think any other candlestick manufacturer in this area can offer a service to match ours. Try us for 30 days and if we are not able to live up to our promise, then you pay us nothing."

Risk reversal No 2: Offer a trial membership: this is just risk reversal by another name. I would say that no brochure for a gym or health club is complete without a free week or month's trial. By including it, you will substantially increase the number of people who are prepared to give you a go, provided certain safeguards are in place.

Order form: Always include either an order form or a choice of ways that your prospect can get in touch with you. If you were sending out a catalogue, you would always include an order form, so when you send out a brochure, why should you do anything different? It always makes sense to give people a 'tick box' option that they can quickly complete and return to you. It then becomes the next logical step in the process.

It's a form of subtle closing that leads your prospects logically into the next part of the buying process. So always include some kind of order form with any brochure – either built in or stapled on as an attachment.

Letter of introduction: When sending your brochure out, always include a letter. You would never dream of starting a sales presentation without introducing yourself first. Similarly, you should never put a brochure in an envelope without an explanatory letter. It needn't be long, but it should further personalise the message that you have put across in the brochure.

A typical introduction may thank the reader for their enquiry, and then mention something specific that you talked about during a phone call for example. This can also give you the opportunity to highlight a particular part of the brochure ("See our special '2 for the price of 1' offer on page 3") that you feel would be of particular interest to the prospect. You have gone to a great deal of hard work to produce an outstanding brochure that speaks directly to your customer. Don't ever send it out without a friendly, personalised letter to accompany it.

There are rules for driving. At first, learning how to control your car and manoeuvre safely may seem complicated, but after some practice, it makes sense why the rules are there. Most people are not aware of any rules when it comes to designing a brochure. They will copy a bit of something they like here with a dash of something that appears to have worked in the past there.

This is how most people go about it, but now you have a far better understanding of how some fundamental marketing principles can be applied to increase your response.

As an example, because you now know the importance of faces on the cover of a magazine, you can double the number of people who will open your brochure. Because you understand what typefaces to use, you can increase the understanding of what you have written by a factor of four.

Most significantly, if you apply all of these ideas and elements together, imagine how much more likely you are to sell your products and services to a prospective customer.

Pre-Launch Checklist – Brochures and Leaflets

☐ Your cover must make a big impact. A combination of an arresting picture and a benefit-driven headline works best.

☐ If you operate in four different sectors, it's better to have a shorter brochure for each sector than one large brochure that tries to cover all of them.

☐ You need to explain what you do, but a brochure is not usually there to close the sale – rather to get people interested enough to call you up. Don't feel that your text needs to explain everything about your company. Too much text will generally put people off, so lay out your pages so that they contain a good balance between text, images and space.

☐ Can your brochure contain any 'added value' content' that will make people hang onto it longer? For example, a salary survey, some tips or useful reference diagrams? Could you even consider using a tips booklet or similar instead of a brochure altogether?

☐ Do the pictures you use have benefit-led captions? People will stop and look at interesting pictures. Giving each a caption that explains a reason why they should use your business is a great opportunity to put a favourable message across.

☐ Make sure that you give all your contact details in the brochure several times. Make it as easy as possible for people to get in touch with you.

Chapter 4

Better results with direct mail and e-mail

- *When to use direct mail* • *Letters vs e-mail*
- *The headline* • *Key elements of direct mail* •
The offer •

The most effective way to communicate directly with targeted customers and prospects.

While a TV commercial, press advert or radio spot is essentially the same message seen or heard by thousands of people simultaneously, a direct mail or e-mail campaign is far more targeted. For a start, it is sent to an individual (either at their home address or their company's). But perhaps most importantly, your letters or e-mails can be carefully targeted to the individuals on your list. You can identify and break down your message according to the sector, size, location or any other important factors that would affect the potential customer you are targeting. Unlike a mass communication medium such as radio or

TV, you are far more accurately able to pinpoint a small cluster of people – and address their interests or concerns directly.

This chapter looks at techniques you can use to write to these people on your database – whether it has been bought in, or compiled by yourself over time. This chapter is mainly about direct mail letters, but most of the ideas equally apply to mail campaigns. The key is to make your communication as individual as possible. You may be contacting thousands of people but you are giving the impression of doing it by writing to one person at a time – and each individual should know it.

When to use direct mail

Direct mail is great for launching a new idea, product or service to targeted groups of people. Direct mail requires a problem (preferably specific) to be addressed or solved. It works best if you target a potential customer likely to be having that problem. For example, if you are launching a new finance product aimed at small companies which you have identified as having cash flow problems, or companies that are approaching the end of their first year of business with a free banking offer, or people who live in houses prone to flooding with a new insurance product, then direct mail is perfect. Direct mail allows you to write to the appropriate person within an organisation, at the right time, and be specific with the information you give them.

Keeping focus in your letter: Whichever approach you use, it is important to remember that the communication should not be just about you or your company. You should aim to make a clear and specific statement about how you can help the person receiving the letter. How you can save them time or money or assist them in saving materials? Can you improve their overall profits and help them meet their business objectives?

If you write to people about these sorts of subjects, can you see why you are more likely to capture their interest than if you simply tell them about what a great company you own? Explain to them how you can help them in their specific situation and you will have a letter that has the attention of the reader. Tell them all about how wonderful your company is and you are quickly heading for the bin.

In addition, it is important to focus on one central message. You can add other advantages later, towards the end of the letter, and give some background about your business, but initially your letter should be focused on one specific area, offer or advantage.

Why direct mail works

Direct mail or e-mail communications work best when you are able to identify a specific, real and current problem and suggest a solution to it. You're communicating with somebody directly – from you to them – and making a compelling case for an answer to a problem they face. If your argument grabs their attention and then talks to them in their language about their problem, you have a much higher chance of getting a response from the prospect.

Don't confuse what we're discussing with junk mail or SPAM, which are inefficient methods of 'spraying' a message to everybody in the hope that it will appeal to somebody out there. This is not something that you should engage in. The better targeted the message and the better crafted the offer, the better the results you will achieve.

With results in mind, one of the many great advantages of direct mail and e-mail is that they allow you to accurately measure the results they achieve. If you send out 1,000 letters, you can and should always measure how many of these people e-mailed, called or faxed you back with a request for more details. By testing out variations of your message, you can improve the effectiveness of your campaign week by week. Once we changed just four words in a headline and tripled the response rate that a letter generated. There are many aspects of direct mail to take into consideration when monitoring effectiveness. Here are some that are worth testing:

- list of names it is sent to
- headline
- time of year / month / week
- offer
- copy inside the letter
- supporting material
- references quoted
- envelope
- follow-up method
- timing of the offer.

Direct mail vs. e-mail

Traditional direct mail letters are a quick and cheap way of getting a message out compared to other marketing media - but slower than e-mail. With direct mail, you can include more material and more details. You have a physical presence in their home/office. You can send your message to named people or simply a job title and it is just as likely to reach the right person. It is more expensive to send than e-mail, but can be used to start the marketing process.

With e-mail, a cold list tends to elicit a poor response so it is more worthwhile to send it to people who have opted in – agreed to receive messages from you either in person or by signing up via your website. It is astonishingly fast to send out and free or very low cost, but response rates are generally far lower as people get inundated with e-mails every day. At the moment, for every letter you receive, you are likely to get around 20 e-mails. In order to make an impact with e-mail, it's best to make it look as much like a 'normal' e-mail as you can.

My recommendation is to use direct mail if you are writing to prospects within companies with which you have no relationship. Once you have met somebody or started some form of communication and they know who you are, then e-mail can be a much cheaper way to stay in touch. Also some organisations such as schools, GPs or hospitals are (for the moment anyway) generally quite bad at using e-mail compared to many private companies.

What to say in direct mail?

There are various things that you can write in your letter that will make it more widely read, but bear in mind that about 50 per cent of people will never even open your letter, so please don't ever expect a 100 per cent response rate. The more you can make your letter look like a personal communication from one person to another, the better.

Here are some questions to ask yourself and some tips to help improve the response rates from the remaining 50 per cent.

The offer: What do you want to say? Why are you contacting these people in the first place? You should always have a reason for writing to people. Is it something new that they can have? Is it a special offer or a reduced price, a new item in stock for a limited time? Whatever it is, the offer is probably the most important area. Getting that right will give you the best start.

Make your offer as eye catching and imaginative as possible. Make it time sensitive and difficult to say 'no' to. Make it believable and above all make it easy to understand. To assess whether you've achieved that understandability, show your letter to a stranger; they should be able to say in about five seconds what you are telling them about if you are to have a chance of winning over people with your direct mail letter.

The headline: This is your best chance to grab the reader and stop them from throwing your letter in the bin. So ask yourself if your headline will stop people doing what they are doing and want to find out more about you. You can't sell to people if you haven't got their attention. You have only three to five seconds to catch people's attention and gain their interest.

The headline should be lively, relevant to the subject that follows and imply a benefit. Look how newspapers use headlines. They use them grab our attention and make us want to find out more. They also signal the type of stories that you will find inside.

The headlines they use actually sell the papers. (It's the same with magazines – the right photo and headline combination can double sales of a title.)

A good headline will stop you as you cross the petrol station fore-court or pop in to the corner shop when you buy your milk in the morning. Then once you have bought the paper, each story headline sells each individual story.

If you don't have a clear benefit-driven headline at the start of your letter, you can wave goodbye to about half of your readers, so spend time getting it right. It has to appeal to your perfect customer so think up a series of headlines that sum up what the letter is about. Create at least 10. I will often write as many as 100 headlines for a client and then test out around four to get the best possible chance of finding a headline that works.

The copy: Which do you find easier to read – Chaucer or *The Sun*? My guess is that, while we may hate to admit it, *The Sun* will win every time. I'm not suggesting that you copy their writing style, but elements of it are admirable. It's clear what they are about. They use short, punchy sentences. There is little ambiguity over what is meant and you don't need to re-read any of it because it was clear the first time.

Direct mail letters with bombastic words and complex jargon can only serve to alienate the reader. They do not impress anyone (except perhaps your English composition teacher). You want to use words and a style similar to what you'd use in a conversation that everybody will understand and that people won't stumble over.

One quick way to discover pitfalls that may be contained within your direct mail copy is to read out aloud what you have written and see if any parts make you stumble. If they do, re-write and re-write until the whole letter flows smoothly.

Use of sub-headings to break up the text makes it clear, crisp and easy to understand in a logical smooth flow. Use of a PS at the end of your letter gets attention and gives it a personal look. When it's all written, look at it without reading the words. Is the formatting pleasing to the eye? Does it look like hard work to read? If it does, see if you can break it up with spaces and breaks.

The format: How long should a direct mail letter be? One school of thought says that the more you tell, the more you sell. While I understand this point, I haven't found it to be true. The most effective length and style of direct mail letter I have worked on is no longer than a single sheet of A4.

The mailing 'pack' itself is divided into a single page letter (preferably on headed paper), a response form that can be posted or faxed back to order the product or ask for more information, plus a further letter or sheet with quotes from satisfied customers. In my experience, this three-part mailer generates a high response rate and has more substance to it than a single page. Test it out for yourself and see which variation works best for you.

Other ideas that can increase your response rates

Create interest by being topical: By using a headline from a newspaper (quoting the publication and date) you can show just how up to date your product or offer is. It also makes it clear that your message is based on 'facts' rather than being made up by you to sell things. I've quoted everybody from the prime minister to Sir Alan Sugar in direct mail letters over the years as a way of grabbing the attention of the reader.

Don't give up too soon: It takes seven meaningful points of contact to make the average sale, yet most people give up on direct mail after one letter. Better to create a list of 100 companies that you really want to work with and mail them regularly than to mail 100 different companies every week.

As part of your regular mailing campaign, send cuttings (about you or relevant stories) to your contact to show that you understand the industry and how it works. Mixed in with regular direct mail letters, these FYIs can be very effective.

Timed to perfection: Timing is almost everything. The day your letter arrives has an effect, as does the time of year you send it. Send your letter so that it arrives on a Tuesday. For other matters, think about the time of year that people are most likely to reply. For example, when mailing schools, September seems to be the best month.

Keep it personal: Stamp rather than frank. It looks less industrial and is almost always more cost-effective because although the cost may be higher, the personal touch generates increased response rates.

Follow up: If resources permit, follow up your letter with an e-mail or a phone call. A good direct mail letter that is followed up by phone within a week of being sent will generate a far higher response rate for you.

The novelty factor: 3D mailers and novelties can work IF they are very carefully targeted; the more personal or suited to the contact, the better. For example, a personalised calendar can work well and even if it is expensive, it can prove to be a good investment in the long term if you bear in mind the lifetime value of a customer.

Every letter counts: Qualify your data. It's a pain, but worth calling people on a mailing list prior to writing to them. Make sure that the name you have is up to date and is the right person to contact; otherwise you might as well save your stamp. It's hard to see how writing to somebody who isn't there anymore or isn't in a position to buy from you is going to end well.

Don't stop thinking about tomorrow

Test, test and test again. If you think you have a good product and there is a market for it, then direct mail should work for you. It's just a question of finding the key to unlocking the door, so keep testing out different headlines, offers, lists etc. You'll find one that works for you in the end – it might just take a few attempts to get it right. Remember that when you are testing, check out one thing at a time.

Pre-Launch Checklist – Direct Mail

☐ Make a good hook to grab the reader's attention in just three to five seconds. That is all the time you have.

☐ Keep it focused. Don't try to cover too many points in your letter. Focus on one central benefit and perhaps a secondary one. You don't want to confuse your audience with too many things to think about.

☐ Think like the customer / prospect. Forget about your company as such and think about what you can do to help people and their businesses.

☐ Use direct mail to test new ideas, new products or new messages. You can measure your response carefully before embarking on more expensive media campaigns.

☐ Keep your text short and punchy. Don't use flowery language. Get people's attention and then keep it by appealing to their self-interest.

☐ Even after following all of these rules, you can't guarantee that everything will go right every time. And even a great response can probably be bettered. Take time to reflect on what could be done better and how you can improve each aspect to fine-tune your letters and generate a more fruitful result next time.

Chapter 5

Hidden riches in niche marketing

• How to find a niche market • Why niche marketing is so effective • Opportunities all around • The 5% difference • Appealing to specialist interests •

The easy way to make a quick impression in a new market area and achieve quick market recognition

In this chapter, we will look at niche marketing and how to use it to break into new markets. This is an area in which I've had quite a lot of success over the years, with clients and in my own business. You may find this chapter particularly profitable because not only can targeting niche areas bring you dramatic results, it doesn't involve any extra expense.

It's also a very good way of quickly establishing yourself in a new market. Increasingly the idea of mass market products is falling out of favour with new niche and even super-niche areas proving especially lucrative.

Why niche marketing works so well

In his book *Purple Cow*, Seth Godin argues forcefully the idea that the mass or major brands, as they evolved after the Second World War, are dead. He notes that the technology which created them – mainly the mass market TV audience – has moved on.

If you think back to Britain in the 1970s, you had essentially one commercial television channel. In America in the 1970s, you had three networks: all advertising on television was through those networks. Radio stations were also limited to one regional station covering different regions of the UK with London being allowed two – Capital and LBC.

Over time, with the relaxation of government controls on broadcasting, this increased as regional radio stations came on-stream and, most recently, community radio stations appeared, serving towns often located in gaps in the coverage of larger city stations.

Now, if you're a satellite television viewer, which most of the people watching TV now are, you would struggle to count the number of channels available. There seems to be at least one for every interest, from fishing to films. But despite the huge number of channels, there are no extra viewers or viewing hours. It's the same viewing share of the cake, but split up into ever-smaller slices. So while even a mediocre sit-com from the '70s could command an audience of 12 million viewers, only the elite of mass audience shows such as *Eastenders* or *The X-Factor* can command those numbers in our new multi-channel age.

Radio has expanded in a similar way with stations specialising in every genre imaginable, for anywhere in the world. We can even create our own radio stations playing music we know we like. Technology has had a similar effect on the magazine and publishing industry. Digital publishing and the improvements in these areas mean that virtually any sector can now support its own magazine. Then you look at the Internet and how that technology has changed the way we get our news and advertising messages – it's totally fragmented the market.

Before, if you wanted to get a certain message across, you would book an advertisement on *News at 10* and half the country would be able to see the advert overnight. Now, it's impossible to build a brand that way. Now there are more fragmented, niche brands that appeal to different areas. I'm guessing few if any readers have been in the position of needing to book an advert on the centre spot of *News at 10*, but the point is you don't have to because it's increasingly easy to create a brand within small niche areas. It's increasingly difficult for brands to become nationally known because of the way technology has moved on.

Godin says, "If we want to grow our business and have our brand known, it's easy if you want to be known in niches, but difficult if you want to be known in mass brands. The days of creating a widely known brand quickly without huge expense have almost gone."

That is one of the interesting things about niche marketing: you can go for very specific audiences and areas quite easily because they are special-interest areas.

If, for example, you identified that a problem for anglers was their inability to obtain life insurance because they were engaged in such a dangerous past-time, you could quickly create a niche insurance company/product. They are a significant niche area that is easy to target. There are many angling magazines to advertise in and they even have television programmes and entire TV channels aimed at them. All you need to do is come up with a distinctive and relevant product name – such 'Anglers Insurance Direct' and you've almost got a company established straightaway because you're creating it within a niche market that is currently unable to obtain insurance.

When we took out our first mortgage, my wife was a teacher. At the time we didn't know the first thing about mortgages. We didn't even know the difference between a tracker and a fixed rate. We didn't have a clue if our credit rating was good enough and we weren't sure where to start. The first company we contacted was called Mortgages for Teachers. At the time, we thought obviously they would understand the specific requirements of a teacher and perhaps offer us a better rate. It turned out to be no such thing, but the name was enough to attract our attention and convince us to sign on the dotted line.

Many people sell financial products that specialise in specific sectors, and that is one of the reasons they grow quickly.

The end of the mass audience?

It's harder these days to reach a wider, general audience. Reaching a more targeted audience is much easier. Here's another example. Imagine an electrical goods store, either a national brand or a locally owned one. Its advert says it is No 1 for all electrical goods – and then lists a load of the different things it sells. But what you want is a washing machine for a good price with a guarantee, and you want it this week. What you are looking for is an advert for a company that talks about washing machines and nothing else. At a later date, the company might want to sell you other things if you had a good experience there, but at this initial stage you're interested specifically in washing machines.

That is one of the great things about niche marketing. You are trying to appeal to those in a buying frame of mind. If you're able to persuade them to visit your website or shop, there is a much better chance of selling them a washing machine than the wide variety of electrical goods you sell. So you want to make it very clear that you sell washing machines. You're not trying to talk about all the other things you do, but being specific about the services you offer. In that way, you'll stand out from all the other people trying to get that buyer's attention.

Attract with the specific: Once your customers have had dealings with you, it's much easier to sell them other products or services. Initially it's about getting their attention. The best way to get the attention of someone buying a washing machine is to tell them about the specific offer you have at the time and your whole line of washing machines. Then you become a niche player for that customer. At a later stage you can tell them about the 30 or so other products you sell, and all because they bought one product from you at first.

At the point of contact, people are usually looking for advice from an expert, to buy something specific or to solve a particular problem they have. They aren't interested at the moment in the fact that you do all sorts of different things. The only thing they want to do is replace their broken washing machine at the best price guaranteed and that's why they'll come to you. They're in a buying frame of mind and if you come across as being the person who can help them, they'll happily talk to you.

Cost implications: One of the arguments people often have when it comes to niche marketing is the cost implications. "I have marketing material produced already for all my major products. Surely if, instead of marketing everything to everyone, I have to come up come up with lots of different campaigns for different products, it will be more expensive." The answer is yes and no. There is a cost but it is actually relatively inexpensive to get different copies of brochures done in comparison to the extra sales it will generate.

For example, a client of mine was about to create a brochure, but when we looked into his market, he was selling this product to extremely different sectors. The product was a cleaning solution for leather which got rid of the nasty infections and odours that can potentially come out after the cleaning process. Essentially, he sold his product into three distinct markets:

- sofa manufacturers in China
- cleaners
- airlines.

The Chinese sofa manufactures had a problem with smell. The sofas were shipped by sea to the UK. It was a long journey from Asia through the Suez Canal and the Mediterranean. Conditions were hot and humid, which encouraged the growth of bacteria that gave the leather foul smells. Around one in 10 sofas had to be thrown out before they reached UK stores.

For the cleaners, after a little research we decided to advertise the product to them on the basis that they would win more contracts because they could clean offices better. The airline customers needed a cleaner to remove the fungus and the different bacteria that tend to grow on leather seats in airlines, so this is how we advertised it to them.

Originally, the client wanted me to do one brochure that covered all of those areas. You can probably see why this is not such a good idea. You simply can't do it because you're looking at distinct sets of problems, different markets, and even slightly different products. We wound up renaming the product in each case to advertise to each of the markets.

In that situation, we did three brochures. The cost was not quite 20 per cent more than he would have paid for a single brochure. For an extra 20 per cent, he got three brochures – each one targeted at a different market and in fact the product went on to become a success in all three markets.

In the brochures for cleaners, we created a 'club' for those who used the products. Membership in the club allowed them to place a special logo on their websites that attested to their ability to eliminate bacteria from office furniture. This demonstrated responsibility on the part of those companies by using the product which proved to be extremely effective in helping them with their real problem – winning new clients.

With a little thought, you can 'nail your niche' without any additional cost. When I won the Marketing Company of the Year award, we didn't even have the money for a brochure. So all we did was print some headed paper with a specific tagline on it. We needed to get new headed paper anyway so there was no extra cost.

When you're thinking about creating extra sections in websites, there might be extra cost implications, but most of the time it's not that difficult to do. What you do may have a minimal cost implication but is worth doing because you'll make that money back through the additional business you will win because of it.

How to find a niche market

So how do you find a niche market? Here are some ways to begin:

Look for a pattern: The easiest way is to look at existing customers and see if a pattern emerges. You might find a particular town, village, or area. Market Harborough, for example, has various areas that are quite wealthy. If I were running a carpet shop there, I might notice we were getting more business in that area, in which case we might run a special advert or promotion for that area.

More commonly you will find your customers come from a specific age group, hobby or special interest group. If you offer five different services, you might be able to look through the selection and determine that half of the people you sell to are requesting information about one of them. So you might consider doing something special for that one area. Promoting it that way might reward you with other business in general.

It's all about looking at the data you have for trends that are of interest to you and considering how you might replicate them at another date.

Ask around: Ask your customers, people around your area or potential customers if there's something they seem to be concerned with or problems you can help alleviate. Ask their opinion on different things and target those markets.

Check the news: Is there a topic in the news you can adapt your product to work for? A company I used to work for made just such a hot topic work for them. It was a telecoms company and made voice mail systems for different businesses, universities, police forces etc. There was a lot of news about truancy in schools and the problems and crime related to it. There were also many reports at the time about the number of kids who weren't in school – something like a million incidents of truancy over the course of a year in England and Wales. It was an extraordinary number.

The research traced it back to kids getting away with it in the beginning. The students would miss a lesson and because it wasn't detected, they would miss another. Then they would miss one or two more in the week. After that there was a snowball effect. Students found out they didn't get caught if they skipped lessons, so they would just carry on doing it.

We developed a text messaging-based product that enabled the school, the first time a child didn't attend registration, to send the parents or guardians a recorded message or a text message from the teacher to report that their child hadn't attended school that day. They were asked to phone the school office to explain why. The mere introduction of the system had an effect on reducing truancy. Instantly, fewer children attempted to play truant because they knew they were going to get caught straightaway. In some cases, attendance rates rose between 10 and 20 per cent because students knew they were going to get caught.

The reason we introduced it was that, while we didn't have any experience in that area, there was a lot of news coverage about it. We spoke to schools where head teachers told us it was a problem and how great it would be if there was a way of solving the problem. The product we introduced was called Informer for Schools, and 95 per cent of it was based on an existing product. We adapted it by changing the name and introducing certain abilities to integrate with schools' registration software programmes. Other than that, it was a product we'd had for a number of years.

That was an example of trying to find a new niche market. We had done a bit of research to find what people's problems were and introduced the technology to help solve that particular problem.

Another example showing the value of market research involves a company that makes flapjacks. Our market research involved asking people on the street what they thought about flapjacks. Their answers revealed something interesting which I hadn't been aware of. It seems a fair number of marathon runners eat them at the halfway point in a race and use them as part of their training regime if they're doing lots of distance running because the oats in the bars contain complex carbohydrates. This amounts to slow energy release, similar to the effect of eating porridge. Our client had never considered marketing to this group before, but there were enough people who ran to make it very profitable.

These are just three of the many ways to find a niche market:

look at your existing customer base, look at market research and find the hot topics in the news. If something is a genuine concern to people, there might be an opportunity for you to create a special niche to address that problem.

Why niche marketing is effective

What is it about niche marketing that works so well? If I were looking to work with someone, who would I want to work with? If I want my attic converted would I choose someone who does general building work, like a general contractor, or do I want to work with a specialist in loft conversions? If I have a bad back, I don't want someone who just works in general massage: I want a person who specialises in sports massage or somebody who specialises in relieving back pain. It's fairly obvious. You want to work with someone who knows what they're talking about.

People often think that by trying to appeal to everyone they'll have a larger audience. In fact, the opposite is true. You wind up appealing to no one because you aren't saying anything specifically helpful. It's much better to divide up the audience into different areas and create a different message for each of those areas.

We want to work with someone who, all other things being equal, presents specific knowledge about a particular area. So rather than going to a generalist, we want to know that the person working for us is an expert in their field.

When you walk into a room and shout, "Hey!" you find a lot of people will look around. But if you instead say, "Bridget, I think I found a way to increase the profits at your nursery..." she will be very interested in what you have to say. You're much more likely to get business from her and get her attention, than if you walk in and say hello to everyone. It may be polite and courteous, but all you're doing is making people vaguely aware that you're in the room and have greeted them. It is much better to find out who specifically is in the room and address their particular needs and problems.

Success stories of niche marketing

How we got major radio station contracts: I want to go into detail in several examples to explain how each of these things work. The first example involves a premium rate phone company. When we started working with them, we quickly realised that our volumes made it impossible to compete with other companies that set up premium rates. With phone-in competitions, half the cost of the call goes to the telecoms company. The other half is split between the radio or television station, or the competition provider, and the company that's providing the line. Typically the split is largely in favour of the company running the competition while the organisation providing the phone lines might get five per cent. You have to operate in large volumes to make any money.

It became clear from Day 1 that we couldn't compete on price with the large premium rate phone line companies. They were placing vast volumes of business with the cable and wireless companies of the world and were able to negotiate extremely cheap rates. So we looked around and came up with the idea of doing something for radio stations.

Commercial radio stations love the idea of the public entering competitions they run. They like to put their listeners on air and have people sounding excited when they win a prize. The problem they had, and the problem that made the niche work, is that a lot of radio stations are very small and have only one or two people on reception at the best of times to cover the phones. In the morning during the breakfast shows, there's usually one person in the production room who answers all the calls, as well as producing the show, making sure the news is run on time, queuing the music for the announcer and so on. It's very difficult for producers to handle this peak volume of work.

We worked out a way of allowing the public to phone a specific number where their calls were recorded. The producer was able to access the recorded calls, go through them to find someone who they could put on air, and phone that person back. Firstly, this was a lot less work for the producer, which was a good thing – if you can make less work for people, it is always appealing. Secondly, the competitions that they were running weren't making any money although potentially they could have been making hundreds of pounds a day. Lastly, it made running competitions a lot easier for the radio station to do.

We got the stations interested with a special report we wrote and then set the phone lines up. After a very short period, around a third of all the commercial radio stations in the UK were using us to run their competitions. That meant we were getting vast volumes of calls coming through our network.

The reason they chose us wasn't because we were experienced in this area, because we weren't. It wasn't because we shared a better portion of call revenue with them, because we didn't. The reason we did so well was because we positioned ourselves as being the company that specialised in radio stations. Rather than trying to reach the thousands of companies that could use the service, we geared all advertising and marketing to the commercial radio industry.

We got some heavy paper printed with the company name and the strapline 'Serving the Radio Industry.' We wrote the special report for the radio industry. We advertised on radio, magazines and websites and sent e-mails. We generally made ourselves known to the radio community. As a result, instead of taking years to establish ourselves, within months we had that third of all the commercial radio stations as clients. We found this niche, worked hard at it, and became very successful.

Eventually we won a major national radio station contract and on a good day we were receiving around 30,000 minutes of call a day - far more than the company had turned over previously. It worked well for us because we became "experts" in this area.

One of the things that helped us in the initial stages was to offer the service free for a few people as a trial to show them how effective it was. After that it was easier to get other people on board because we were able to point to some successful examples.

Incoming telephone queuing system for healthcare industry niche: Another good example comes from a company I worked with that resells phones. This company re-badges phone systems and sells them on to schools, colleges and other institutions. It has been around for a long time and has grown steadily over the years with a wide client base.

One day, the MD had a problem contacting the doctor for his child, who had a fever. He couldn't get through on the phone: it was permanently engaged. When he spoke to other people, it became clear that this was a fairly common experience. It was almost impossible to reach your doctor between 8:15 and 9am because everyone was trying to get through at that time.

So the company took what was a fairly standard piece of equipment, rebundled it with around 15 other items such as call recording, panic buttons and headsets and offered it with an 0844 number to enable virtual queuing. This meant that patients would always be able to get through to the surgery or could queue until someone was available to speak to them. The company worked out a way to do it so that people queued on average for less than 90 seconds before having their call answered.

It was a controversial system but it became phenomenally successful. At the time of writing is being used by about 2,000 surgeries in the UK and as there are around 9,000 surgeries in the country, more than 20 per cent of the surgeries in Britain are clients. That is actually more than all of the other clients in all the other sectors they operate in that they acquired over the previous 25 year period! This is because, instead of trying to 'spray' market to everyone, it focused on one sector – GPs. Our PR was aimed at doctors' magazines and all the effort was focused on one area to get repeat business, so the company become well-known in that area.

This is one of the benefits of niche marketing. Even if you have a limited budget, if you've done your homework and discovered where there is a genuine need, you'll quickly be picked up and become known in that sector. .

A gym focuses on a specific market segment: This is a fictional example. Suppose you've set up a gym and you want people to join it. You could do general marketing saying, 'Join this gym.' Or you could go into a local magazine aimed at the 50+ crowd and offer something special for that market. Or you could aim at those under 20, those looking to lose weight, or a different promotion for those who are about to get married. There are many different promotions you could go for, aimed at specific areas. Alternatively, you could base your promotions around the success of local magazines in your area, or make your adverts in the local press aimed at a specific segment of the market.

A maintenance company does niche marketing: A maintenance company once used a very general advert in the local newspaper. This was changed a number of years ago to say specifically that it was a specialist in central heating systems and servicing boilers. Its business has dramatically grown as a result. It has twice as many engineers on the road now as it did five years ago. That is because it specialises. The company is profitable, has a reputation for doing central heating and boilers and is very good at it. It still handles other maintenance work but rather than advertising everything it can do, it goes for this one area and as a result gets more enquiries.

Sky TV used niche marketing for big business: In case you think this is something for small businesses only, it's not. A great example of this is Sky TV. It has close to 10 million households – that's a pretty wide market. Sky does general advertising that appeals to everyone, but the way it's grown is not only by having this wide blanket coverage, but also going after specific niches.

One of the ways it got going in the early days was through sport. Its directors knew people were passionate about football, rugby or cricket; they wanted to watch these events and were prepared to pay for them. So Sky put together a more comprehensive sports package than had previously been available. The channel used premiership football and other top sporting events as a way of getting people to sign up in the first place. Over time people have enjoyed various other programmes like The Simpsons, but they went for programmes that already had a big audience. Sky's advertising was aimed at football magazines or film magazines; it would advertise specific areas of the overall service. That's how the channel attracted customers in volume, by going for a selection of niche areas.

Most people who sign up for Sky do so for specific reasons. Often, it is as simple as the fact that they want to see England play the West Indies in the winter, or whatever. They sign up for that initially and then stay customers as they discover the other services that Sky offers. So, even a massive organisation like Sky uses niche marketing all the time and finds it's a much more effective way to get customers to sign up.

How to make niche marketing work for you today

Are you thinking about how niche marketing would work for you? Firstly, consider your existing clients and see if there are some examples of how you have helped them in particular ways. This can be a sector starting point. If you've identified that you've worked with a lot of garden centres or garage mechanics for example, you may have identified a trend. You might have a group of customers who use you a lot, and who are loyal, dependable customers. That's probably a great place to start.

Now go into a bit more detail. How have you actually been able to help these people? See if you can find some clear examples of how you've been able to save them money /save time/ make life easier for them. Put together case studies or testimonials that you can share with other companies in their sector so that it's clear how you are able to help that particular type of company.

You can also look at renaming your product (e.g. Anglers Insurance Direct) to specifically service that sector; even if the product remains essentially the same as before. Choosing a name relevant to a particular niche will draw customers to you and help position you as a leader in that field.

Consider if it was a stop-smoking product and you wanted those particular people who were identified as your niche market to take notice. Maybe you notice that there are certain times of the year when people try to stop smoking, such as National Stop Smoking Day. Could there be a name for your product that would help people stop smoking now? It might be what you have been doing for years, but coming up with a specific product for it would give people a way of grabbing on to it. Alan Carr had a brand called 'The Easy Way...' which became a generic term and was popular for product launches. But it started off as 'The Easy Way to Stop Smoking': there wasn't actually anything different about that product except that it let people know it was easy. Could you re-label your product in a way that would be specific to the market you are aiming for?

Once you've done that, you can really go to town and start

sending out press releases for that sector. You can create detailed case studies or a specific brochure for that sector. You can create some heavy paper just for that sector. These are simple, easy, low-cost things you can do that will concentrate your focus on one relatively small sector. What that means is that rather than trying to get thousands of businesses vaguely interested in what you do, you know there are a few hundred that are VERY interested in what you do because they can see clearly how you are able to help them.

Pre Launch Checklist – Niche Marketing

Niche marketing can be a very effective way of launching a new business or relaunching an older company that needs a new direction because it concentrates activity on a small area of the market. By focusing your attention on one area you concentrate your efforts, awareness and results.

It's also free, or virtually free to use. It costs no more to print a 'police focused brochure' than a general brochure, but the response you will generate from the police will be far higher than you would have had by sending them a general brochure.

You can get quicker results online. To get to the No 1 position on Google with the term 'recruitment company' would be hard, but if you wanted to get to No 1 with the term 'retail recruitment Birmingham', it is going to be much easier and bring you far more qualified and relevant visitors.

People prefer to deal with a specialist rather than a jack of all trades. They prefer coming to experts who know about their particular problems. When you understand the specific problems people have within a particular industry – and make it clear that this is an area of your expertise – then you rise above the competition. This automatically adds value to your service and you can rise above price wars and charge a premium for your specialist knowledge.

☐ Niche marketing can be applied to every other area of this book, and in fact every area of marketing. From direct mail to PR, from branding to press advertising, if you focus on different niche areas and how you can solve those specific problems, your enquiries and sales will increase.

☐ The more specific you can be about the benefits you are able to offer people from different niche areas, the more successful you will be in the long run,

Chapter 6

Harnessing the power of the Internet

• Purpose of a website • First impressions • Content checklist • Website optimisation • Links and how they work • Power of the blog • E-mail marketing and newsletters to generate traffic to your site •

> Make the most of the biggest change in generations in the way people research and buy products.

Your company may already have a website. You may even have a website that you are actually very happy with that generates new business for you. Or you may be an Internet beginner. Either way, this chapter will be useful. It will help if you are thinking of creating a site from scratch or can't figure out why you don't seem to be receiving enquiries, or don't seem to come up in the appropriate section in search engines. This chapter can become a kind of checklist to ensure that your Internet marketing takes off.

What is the purpose of your website?

Websites have come a long way from the early days of the world wide web when the majority were simply an online brochure. This was how most people saw the usefulness of websites in the mid-1990s, when people and organisations started building them for the first time. If a company already had a brochure or a catalogue, it would use the exact same contents, photographs and often even the same design to create its website.

Much has happened in the fast-moving, innovative technology behind the Internet. As a result, websites have moved far beyond that starting point and have become engines of growth for business.

One of the best uses of a website is to generate new business leads. If you chat with somebody at a meeting, you give them your card. If they are in any way interested in what your company does, they look at your website. They will then immediately judge you on a whole range of criteria, consciously or otherwise. Rightly or wrongly, things such as broken links, missing images or out-of-date content will start to raise questions in their mind about what sort of business you run. If your demeanour and presentation says that you run a highly professional, successful business, but your website says:

- 'under construction'
- or it is an amateurish, unprofessional website
- or it is out of date

...then it will probably do you more harm than good. This may be a reason why some introductory e-mails go unanswered and some phone calls aren't returned.

It is worth getting the website right from the beginning as it is a way of generating leads, and also of confirming your reputation. A good website can work for you 24 hours a day and start generating business while you are sleeping. Isn't that great!

A website provides comfort and assurance to a potential customer. It gives confidence that they will be dealing with a clean, professional and healthy company. It is a way for people to see that you are the company that you say you are.

Is the comfort factor increasingly important these days? Yes, credibility is a massive factor now. You may spend a lot of money on promotion, displaying web addresses on vans and advertising in magazines. But if people then enter your website and find information that is five years or more out of date, your company's credibility is shattered.

Put yourself in their position. When you go onto a company's website and the lead news item – sometimes the only news item – reads 'ABC Ltd launches new website 2004', your heart sinks. You are left thinking, "Is that the best they can do?" You regret having wasted your time in opening that website and move swiftly on.

Things to consider when designing your website

The design of the website needs to be 'fit for the purpose' of that company. It needs to be suitable for the job. If you are a serious business-to-business service, your site must reflect this. If you are renting a holiday cottage, then your site should reflect this with colours, text and pictures all reflecting holiday makers' needs.

And that's not all. In 2005, Google estimated that people would tolerate 15 seconds for a page to open. In 2009, it was down to three seconds. If your website is badly optimised with a heavy load of graphics and takes more than 15 to 20 seconds for just the first page to open, you won't even have a chance to make the first impression. The potential customers will have gone faster than they came.

A website must also be easy to navigate. If someone visiting your site wants to contact you, they shouldn't have to make their way through a maze to do so. Website users should not require a PhD or a degree in rocket science to find the contact form! Ensure the website is clear, nice and clean – and easy to access.

In terms of first impressions, what do you want people to do when they reach your site? It's worth making a list of how you think people will use the site. Think about the most important sections. A good idea is to plan a route; think of a retail environment where a path has been designed to take people through a shop following a specific logic. A website could use the same concept and lead visitors along a route that will result in lead generation and sales.

A common mistake that many people make is to leave things that don't work on their site. You come across these every day – images that won't load, links that don't go anywhere, pages that just fall over or freeze. You can avoid that by making someone responsible for checking the site daily. That's far better than waiting for someone to send an e-mail informing you that part of your site doesn't work. By the time that happens, a large number of potential customers will have already turned their backs on you.

Your first page should contain something new and topical and give the impression of a forward-thinking company where things are constantly being updated. Having a 'news section is a good idea; or a special offer. This is something that separates old websites from new ones. In the past, it was expensive to change content, whereas now it is very easy and inexpensive to update a website. Nowadays you can update company websites internally – especially the blog pages – to keep the site fresh.

Contents and appropriateness

Make your website about how you can help your prospective customer. Tell them about specific cases where a customer's needs were more than met; quantify that customer's gain. Anticipate what generally ails the industry in which you operate and spell out what exactly you will do to offer customers a solution.

It's amazing how many sites fall into the same old trap – it's all we, we, we. 'We do this and we do that', and the whole home page has information about when a company was formed and how great the founders were, to the point of sycophancy. This is of absolutely no interest to the visitor at the early stage.

If you look at the very successful websites, they usually go straight into the benefit for the customer or specifically what they are selling. Amazon, the biggest online retailer in the world, immediately has information on books and CDs that are likely to interest you – not how big the company is. It may have that type of information somewhere, but Page 1 contains a list of the latest books and special offers to immediately hook you in.

At the other end of the scale, Andrew Bourne and Company is

an insurance broker in Leicester who I have recently been helping – *www.abourne.com*. It has the specific specialist sectors on the front page of its site so as soon as you hit it, you can start looking for information of the type of insurance that interests you.

You need to remember that you have just a few seconds to hook people and get their interest. So make sure your home page is as welcoming and interesting as you can possibly make it.

Remember that people will not read huge amounts of text online. They don't mind seeing a lot of text, but don't expect them to read it. Keep it clean and simple. Avoid using odd fonts on the screen. Use headings and sub-heads that make the main points you want them to understand. If you do have a lot of information you want to get across and there isn't a way of cutting it down, then make a series of bullet points, so that you have clarified what you think they would be most interested in.

Once you have made the key points, by all means explain in a little more length, but in doing this, concentrate on the key phrases that are likely to be picked up by the search engines.

If you wish to get across your expertise or credibility early on, then the use of testimonials can work well. Testimonials are always worth gathering in; you can sprinkle them all over your website, so that you have other independent voices singing your praises. I saw an unusual website which had nothing but testimonials on the main page. They hook visitors and make them curious to see what makes this company tick so loudly.

In short, when people visit your site you are often a stranger to them. Testimonials increase people's confidence in what you do.

Captions for pictures are also very important. If you have a caption underneath a photograph, it works in a couple of different ways. It not only helps Google search engines to find the content of your website, but if you have a benefit led caption under your photo, it's another way of getting a benefit across.

For example, a typical photo caption might be:

Alastair Campbell, MD of The Ideal Marketing Company

However a far better caption would be:

Alastair Campbell, MD of the Ideal Marketing Company, hosts marketing seminars and runs a marketing mentoring service for business owners

The second caption uses 'marketing seminars and 'marketing mentoring' – two key search engine phrases that I optimise my website for.

People do notice pictures and quickly look underneath to scan the caption. Don't waste this opportunity to put across a key message about your business.

As a general rule, the sentences used in your site should be short and punchy. Don't waffle on. You want to keep what you say brief and factual. People have a fairly short attention span at the best of times. Online, they search quickly, scanning for what they want to see and moving on if they don't find it. Visitors are probably going to be zooming up and down on your website and aren't likely to read everything, so keep the contents short and crisp. Use key phrases and be straightforward about what you are trying to get across.

Avoid complicated humour or anything that would be easy to

misinterpret. Keep it simple and benefit led – remember, what's in it for them?

Website optimisation

Optimisation is like goal-setting for your website. You need to be clear who it is you want landing on your site from Day 1. Create your site around some key phrases and aim it at your defined audience.

It is important to be clear about which phrases your customers will use to find you. At times you can get too focused on what you do and lose track of what people want, which determines the words they will be searching under. People search in different ways, so think about the solution they may be seeking, rather than the product you offer.

Take NLP (neuro-linguistic programming) training as an example. Some people know the term NLP, but others just know that they want to solve certain problems in their life. So there are two ways to optimise a site offering this training methodology. The first is simply to use terms around NLP; the other is to use typical phrases associated with the results from the courses offered. So people searching for the solution to 'how to deal with difficult staff' would find the site as well as these searching for 'NLP problem solving'.

Think about what phrases people might use to find your services or longer phrases around what you do that people might key in. This is just the starting point because next I am going to tell you about a very useful tool to see what people are really searching for – and it's free.

Key word suggestion

Google actually offers this great tool called the 'key word suggestion tool'. If you have not heard about it before it will be quite a revelation to you. To find it, go to Google and do a search for 'Key word search tool' where you will find it as part of 'Ad-Word programme'. You can enter a phrase that you think your customer might use and the tool will tell you how many searches using that phrase were carried out over a period of time. It will also tell you other similar phrases that were searched. This is a clever tool that few people use or know about, but which has the potential to make a huge difference to your website traffic. Instead of creating your site around a phrase that nobody is searching for, you can alter text on your site to match more popular searches – and find your traffic doubles within weeks.

Here's an example from one of my own websites – *www.themarketingmentor.co.uk*. We originally optimised for the term 'marketing mentor'. After using the Google key word suggestion tool, we found that three times as many people searched under the term 'marketing mentoring' (an expression we'd never used). There were also a number of suggestions (12 in total) in a similar vein. So we now use a lot of these phrases when updating the blog on the site. In fact, when some terms in the blog were changed, the number of people visiting the site almost doubled in the space of just over a week.

So, just by spending a bit of time researching what key words people are using, you can optimise your website to become much more effective. If you don't do this, you could find, as Stephen Covey said in his book *7 Habits of Highly Effective People*, that you have to spend a lot of time climbing up a ladder on one side of a building, only to discover that you actually climbed up the wrong building.

Blogs

One of the biggest changes in the last couple of years in how we use the Internet is in the area of blogs and how they are instrumental in getting your website found.

A blog (from the term 'web log') is a type of online journal or diary. It's a way of showing your site is kept up to date, but mainly it is the best possible tool to make your site visible to search engines.

Researchers in America found that, in the corporate sector, stories in a blog were picked up quickly by Google. Because Google is biased toward new material on the web, news is at the top of the searches. You can write a blog story and get on the first or second page of Google very quickly.

If you want to be listed under Valentine's chocolates delivery, then you simply start using this term in your blog entries as a heading of the stories you are creating and file them in a special section on your site. The result? Within a few weeks, you are likely to be on Page 1 for even a fairly hotly contested term.

The blog software I would recommend is a package called Word Press www.wordpress.com. It's web-hosted software that can be added to an existing site. It's very easy to use. It works as a content management system, so wherever you are, you can log in by username and password to maintain a story.

Blogs allow you to react quickly to something that is

happening TODAY that is relevant to your customers. This is one area where a website is streets ahead of a brochure. You can talk about an exhibition you attended, a breaking news story, even about a member of staff leaving or someone who is pregnant in the accounts office. All fantastic things to write about because it gives your blog relevance if you know what term people are looking for and can adapt the story so it uses your selected key phrases.

Suitable contents for a blog: A lot of people say that they'd love to have a blog, but they don't know what they'd write about. Here are a few suggestions:

- Firstly, pure marketing content. For some of your posts, you can simply lift a section of text from one of your direct mail letters, part of a brochure or a flyer. Simply re-use the text and add it to your blog.
- Secondly, write about things completely unrelated to marketing. Feature personal stuff about the company: the firm's night out, the golf day etc. These are great 'social' things to write about and help put a human face on your business.
- Thirdly, write about support content. This is giving answers to frequently asked questions (FAQs) around your trade. If you have written a story, it gives you greater relevance and weight within your key word sector. People do write questions.
- Fourthly, read trade magazines or look through trade sites for stories that may be of interest to your

customers. *Do not cut and paste other people's content, however, as this is against the law.* By all means use quotes, reference any statistics and facts, but don't lift stories word for word.

How important are headings in blogs? Always give your blog a heading linked to the terms you want your site to be found under. Start the post with this phrase and then use some extra information about the subject that follows – 'Solar heating Leicestershire – gas bills set to rise again'.

Can you find time to write a blog and keep it up to date? Can you not! A survey recently carried out by the British Management Council found that 70 per cent of business owners in the US have taken to blogging, and they see its worth, compared to only 23 per cent in the UK. At the moment in the UK, we have a resistance to it for some reason, but for people who use blogging properly, the results are significant. The time it takes to update your blog is tiny compared to the results it can generate. Why not get yourself a cup of tea and a sandwich at lunchtime and just type out a blog entry: it only takes five minutes. We should all be able to find five minutes to do that little bit in our business, once a day, or three times a week.

Perhaps part of the resistance to blogging is that, although it's such an important thing, it might feel like you are simply playing around. If we post a direct mail letter and physically put the letters in the post, we can see something going out; as we lick the stamps, we feel that we are doing 'proper marketing'. Somehow in our minds, adding an entry to our blog seems to be just messing around. That needs to change, because it is possibly one of the most useful things you can do in terms of your website. So please seriously consider adding a blog to your site and keeping it updated.

If you really can't find the time or don't know where to start, there are companies or virtual assistants that will work out a brief and keep your blog up to date on your behalf. At the moment, I do this for almost half of my clients, so even if you have to outsource the work, it is possible to have a blog that is generating good quality enquiries on your behalf.

During a recent seminar, I asked how many people in the room had a blog on their company website. There were around 40 business owners present and only two people put their hands up – and I was one of them. It is disappointing that more people aren't seeing this as a great opportunity.

This whole scenario has changed in the last two years. I don't think I even knew what a blog was in 2006, but now I would advise more and more clients to look at it. I can't think of any company that would not benefit from having a blog as a way of keeping their customers informed. It's just a great way of pushing your website up the ranking.

What's interesting is no-one knows how long this is going to carry on, but at the moment it's a potential gold rush for businesses. It's an easy way to get to the top of the search engine listings. It might change in the future, but for now blogs, particularly Word Press blogs, seem to be the thing.

Links - how they work and what they do

Once you've optimised your site for a series of key words and phrases you will find that you start to list on Google but if you want to get further up, what can you do? .

One of the other things that Google looks at is the number of links that are coming into your site. This is not a link that you are giving out, but a link that is coming in. Google counts these links and calculates 'link popularity'. So, if you can get a link coming into your site, it's always good if it is relevant to what you do.

If you say to a friend, "I'll put a link on my web page and you put a link on yours," Google is clever enough to see that and will discount them. A few years ago, people were advised to do this. There used to be a service that we subscribed to called Link Farming; you could go to the website and create a big page of links on your site and those sites would give you a link back. When Caged Fish started eight years ago, we had casinos and all sorts of links into us. Now all the relevance to those links has gone. But it remains important to get as many inbound links as possible.

Another fantastic way of doing this is to comment on other people's blogs and ask other people to comment on yours.

You might wonder if it's such a good idea to ask clients or strangers to comment on your blog. A comment policy is fundamental; basically it allows people to put a comment against your stories. You still have control and you allow whether people's comments finally will go live on your site.

So, if it is something defamatory or simply a junk comment, you simply delete it, but allow appropriate comments.

Yell.com: People are using Yellow Pages less and less, but they do use Yell.com. Is this a good way to spend money? This depends on what you offer. Yell.com can be great for a distressed purchase service, such as a plumber.

The best thing is to be in control of your own destiny and market your own site for your set key words and phrases.

E-mails

Assuming you have a well optimised website, another thing you can do is use the power of e-mails to promote your website. Here are a few suggestions:

- One of the simplest is to make sure that you put a signature at the bottom of your e-mail with contact details, including your website. It's surprising how many people don't. Think how many people you may e-mail in a day who might look at your site as a result. I recently took my family on a holiday and the reason I chose that resort was because of an e-mail the owner had sent me earlier in the year giving feedback on an event I'd help organise.
- It's also a good idea to embed a link into your e-mail in the text that allows people to go straight to the website.

Newsletters

About a year ago, I changed the way I sent out my newsletters. I used to send out a newsletter that had a lot of content. It was all very nicely designed and ran into a couple of thousand words, its articles going into a lot of detail. I've changed it now so that it's no more than three paragraphs, but each paragraph is just the start of an article. So, it has a headline, two or three sentences at the start of the article and if the reader has a further interest, they can click into the blog where further details can be found.

I noticed that in the weeks I send out my newsletter, the traffic to my website generally doubles because people are clicking through to read the rest of newsletter. Once they are on the website, people can start looking at different sections.

So, use newsletters as a way of generating traffic to your website. Get viewers to initially read a story or look at an offer and once people are on your website, the chances are they will stay on and look at what else you do. A great way to get traffic to your site.

Get people to sign up to your newsletter: You don't want people to just look at your website for a while and then go off and look at someone else's site without leaving any information. Consider how you can capture passing traffic. You need something on your website that makes people want to leave their details. Get them to sign up to newsletters, or offer free tips booklets or a free consultation.

Key word tail-off or long tail key words? So many people get frustrated trying to optimise to come up under a one word or two word search phrase. Google did some research last year into how we search. It found that whereas two or three years ago we were searching with two words in a Google search, we are now searching with four, five and six words. But the trick is to look at the bigger picture when you are doing your key word analysis.

I could optimise the words 'marketing seminar' but it is easier to optimise 'marketing seminar, Leicester, marketing seminar, Market Harborough, marketing seminar, Birmingham' because people will actually search with those longer phrases. It is easier to get to the top of longer searches such as these because not a lot of people are optimising for the more specific searches. You can actually sneak up on larger companies by using this key word tail off, if you are in a saturated market.

So, being specific about search terms (and longer search terms) is more likely to lead to success – and easier. This is where the key word suggestion tool mentioned earlier could be used again.

The phrase 'long tail key' was coined by Chris Brown talking about the Amazon business model. Amazon didn't sell a lot of one thing, but they went on to sell lots and lots of little things and they optimise for all these different things.

Images: Images from Google aren't free – so don't use them on your site. It's unethical and you may well get found out. If you inadvertently use a picture that is owned by one of the main picture libraries, you could end up being fined thousands of pounds.

Two great stock image websites are *www.sxc.hu* or *www.istock.com* where you can buy images for as little as £1. *www.sxc.hu* even has a selection of good images that are free to use in certain circumstances – always check the copyright before using an image on your site.

.com vs .co.uk: If you have a .com domain name, it is always worth knowing where your website is hosted, because if you go to Google and do a UK-only search, Google looks at the domain name suffix – .co.uk or .com. If you are .com, it will look at where your site is hosted. If you are a British company with a .com and the site is hosted in America, you won't show up in a UK search. There won't even be a mention of your company.

Watch out for a hosting company called One-on-One.co.uk, a big host which most people assume is a UK company. It's not. At the time of writing this company actually hosts sites from Germany even though its offices are in the UK. If you want to check where a site is actually hosted, call Steve Hawkins at Caged Fish on 01858 46 99 88 and he will be happy to check for you. Steve has also been a major help in writing this chapter and has suggested many of the ideas here.

Copying: It is also against the law to copy from other people's websites. It's theft, pure and simple. If you like the way one of your competitors has written his website, you can't just cut and paste it to your website. This sort of behaviour might sound outrageous, but I've seen people do it several times.

Similarly, if you find an article you think will be quite good in your blog, you can't just take it. However, what you can do is put some of the article on to your blog and then put a link to the complete article. You could use all of it, but you would need to explain clearly where the article came from and who wrote it, list the domain name and put something like "I thought you might be quite interested in the article by..." The writer should not have a problem with this because you are publishing his article and creating a link back to his site. Don't pretend you have written someone's article. You could get into a lot of trouble, plus it is unethical and the person who wrote the article retains the copyright.

Recognition of duplicate content: Also, on an optimisation front, Google has a programme that will recognise duplicate content. So if you swipe a nice bit of content from someone's website, Google will recognise this and ignore it. It is always best to write fresh content using key words.

Shopping demographic: If your company sells online, there is recent research available on how the male and female shopping demographic works. It appears that things have flipped on their head. When it comes to traditional shopping, women tend to take their time – trying things out, looking around – only to come back to the first shop they visited and buy at the end of the day.

Now this is how the man will shop on the Internet. He will go from site to site, get a deal, jump around and then decide where he is going to purchase it.

However, women shop more like a traditional man in a shopping centre. They find a site, see if it seems okay and then buy. This is worth taking into consideration if you are gearing your site towards a female or male market.

What is the law on sending e-mail newsletters to people's addresses and opting in or out? The rule is, if you are sending to a consumer or a member of the general public, they are supposed to opt into your list.

If you are sending to a business, as the law currently stands you are allowed to prospect. If the business says to you that they never want to hear from you again, then you should respect that. Companies prospecting for business have to give an unsubscribe facility in the e-mail.

It is best to build your own list organically, rather than buying a list. The chances are that the list will be wrong, or companies won't be interested in what you do.

Pre-Launch Checklist – Websites

☐ Bear in mind that the first thing many people will see of your business is through your website, so make sure it offers a good first impression.

☐ Keep your content short, simple, easy to read and engaging. Write a lot if you need to but if so, break it up. Go for simplicity where possible as people skim-read text on websites.

☐ Remember your key phrases and optimise your site for these. Repeat them wherever possible and don't be afraid to state simply what you do.

☐ Don't allow your site to grow old. Make sure content is up to date. The simplest way to do that is to add a blog to your site.

☐ Drive traffic to your site by creating links on other people's sites, by using e-mail newsletters and making sure your website is on everything from e-mails to business cards.

☐ Don't steal other people's text or images. By all means study their sites for good ideas, but never steal text or other material. Make your site original, pertinent and something that your company can be proud of.

Conclusion

What next? Are you ready for lift-off?

The late Jim Rohn makes a very important point in his book *7 Strategies for Wealth & Happiness.* He says: "There are always half a dozen things that make eighty per cent of the difference." Somewhere in the preceding six chapters, I hope you'll find your personal 'half a dozen things'.

When I started writing this book, I wondered how I could include ALL the marketing material that you would need. Then I changed my mind. I thought about the books that I like to read. I don't want to wade through dozens of pages to find a useful part. I'd rather read about the six things that make the difference. In this book, I have tried to focus on the half-dozen areas that right now will make the biggest difference to you.

Whether you are a business owner or an astronaut, you will find that success usually comes down to focusing on a small number of fundamentals done well.

Like a rocket on the launch pad, you should find your fuel tanks full, engines primed and all systems ready for lift-off.

Just before I leave you to get on with what I hope will be a long and successful journey, let's part with a few general business thoughts to bear in mind as you start putting the ideas from this book into play.

No matter what the economic conditions, you don't want to be travelling with unnecessary baggage. It uses up extra fuel and slows you down on your mission. And what about your crew: is every member carrying their weight and more? If not, perhaps they should be dropped off along the way.

As you count down for launch, it makes sense to check your trajectory and be clear about where you are heading. Where are you now and where do you want to be in one year, three years or five years time? Imagine yourself at your ultimate destination and work your way backwards. What did you have to do differently in order to get there? If your one-year goal is to win five new clients, then work out a plan that will get you there. How are you going to build that client list? What is the best route to travel in order to reach that destination?

What are your instrument panels telling you? Nobody relies on gut instinct to measure how fast they are going, how much fuel they have on board etc. What evidence do you have that indicates there is demand for new products or a new direction? Do your due diligence. Is there more market share to grab? Have any of your competitors gone under? Is there a growing need for your product or service? Look at your instrument panel to assess whether you're heading in the right direction.

The reason that a man first stood on the moon was to a large extent because of competition between the United States and the Soviet Union during the 1960s. It was political competition that created the 'space race'.

Competition is not a bad thing, especially if it keeps you on your toes. Determine what you have that your competitors wish they could steal from you and look at what they are doing that you are not. Make the most of your strengths and use your marketing to clarify the main competitive advantages that you have to your customers.

It is easy to control a vehicle if the vision of where you are heading is in alignment with where you want to be. Ask yourself if your strategies are aligned with your company's values. If one of your values is to keep your customer happy, then put all the resources you can into making that the company's top priority. Perhaps now is the time to implement that CRM programme to manage your information and amaze customers.

It's great to reach a far-flung destination, but even better to reach it at a specific time. Are you realistic about how long your journey will take? Do you understand the difference between the demanding and the impossible, and can you identify each? It's good to have a realistic strategy that works within an expected time frame. Don't let your excitement blind you to the realities around you. Be rational about how long it will take you. Everything takes time, planning and effort. Make sure that your team is on board and ready to help you make the journey a success.

And remember the words of Steve Chandler in the introduction of this book. This book is about the 'how to'. Before you continue on the journey, make sure you have the 'want to'. If you want to grow, if you want to succeed and if you really want to do it, then this book will help you lift off and to speed up your journey. If you don't really want to, then the chances are slim of reaching any lasting success. Focus first on wanting to and when you are sure you do, this book will help you to do it.

It takes a lot of planning and effort to get ready for the launch. The lift-off uses up most of the fuel, but once you've broken free of gravity and gained momentum, the journey becomes far easier to control.

Enjoy the journey.

Acknowledgements

Working in the advertising and marketing industry for more than 20 years, you get to meet many inspiring, impressive and sometimes scary people. I have learned so much from my many bosses, assistants and work colleagues over the years that I wouldn't know where to begin to acknowledge them all, but Ted Welsh, Garry Durston, Stefan Olsberg, David Harrison, Rebecca Robertson, Ted Nicholas, Earl Nightingale, Nick Robinson, Graham Sayles, Nigel Risner and Steve Chandler have all been inspirational figures who taught me a great deal at different stages of my career.

I am also grateful to all of my clients past, present and future for the opportunity to test out new ideas and for having faith that I know what I'm talking about.

In writing this book, I am indebted to Chuck Grieve for his skill, patience and faith, Steve Hawkins and Garry Aston for their specialist Internet knowledge and to Ashok Gupta for his assistance to reviewing the chapters.

About the author

Alastair Campbell was born in Stirling, Scotland in 1967. He studied Film and Television at Harrow College (now Westminster University) and after graduating, worked for several London advertising agencies during the industry's boom years of the late 1980s and early '90s. During this period he won a national competition for writing a Holsten Pils TV commercial.

After almost 10 years with the Pearson-owned Register Group, during which time he rose to become marketing manager, in 1997 he relocated out of London to Leicestershire. There, as marketing manager for Lines Unlimited, he helped the company win business with almost half of the commercial radio stations in the UK and received the Marketing Company of the Year Award from the Marketing Guild.

After six years with the group, latterly as head of the marketing and telemarketing departments of the firm's holding company, Voice Connect, Alastair left in 2003 to set up The Ideal Marketing Company.

Since then, he has worked for clients in sectors as diverse as print, leisure, recruitment, food, education, IT, retail, motorsport, construction, TV, health, training, skiing, retail, insurance, weight loss, food and packaging. He has always believed that effective, low-cost marketing ideas should be made to work for every business and spreads this message via his seminars and public speaking engagements which have taken him to the NEC, Olympia, the Walkers Stadium,the MK Dons Stadium, Madejski Stadium, The National Liberal Club in Westminster and Hothorpe Hall. He writes for trade magazines and websites and has been a regular contributor to BBC radio since 2002.

Alastair practises what he preaches, working with clients on a consultancy basis – helping them implement many of the ideas contained in this book. In 2008, he set up The Marketing Mentor programme to help companies with their marketing on an on-going basis by using monthly phone conferences and open question sessions.

Alastair and his wife, Helen (who is a fellow director in the company) have two sons at secondary school. They believe it is important to find a balance between work and home life and admit that it's not always easy.

"Marketing," he says, "is about spending time and thought to be clear about what you are hoping to achieve rather than throwing money at it. Do more of what works for you, but do some marketing activity every week without fail to avoid boom and bust in your company."

■ *You can contact Alastair directly with feedback, comments or questions at alastair@idealmarketingcompany.com or by telephone on 01858 44 55 43.*

■ *www.idealmarketingcompany.com*

■ *www.themarketingmentor.co.uk*

The PR Launchpad

Using PR can be a great way to gain positive media coverage
for your company. But understanding what is newsworthy,
how to gain coverage and how to handle media attention is
not always obvious. *The PR Launchpad* explains how to go
about generating publicity for your company in an age of
mass media as well as social networking.

The Sales Launchpad

Whether it is face to face or over the phone, the idea of sales
has negative connotations for many people. In *The Sales
Launchpad*, Alastair Campbell dispels the notion that the 'gift
of the gab' is necessary to sell and offers practical ideas on
how to make the most of our natural abilities to listen, ask
questions and empathise to secure more orders for your
business.

The Marketing Matrix

Every marketing activity has four key components. How much
each is used depends on the stage a company is at and its
strategy for growth. In *The Marketing Matrix*, Alastair
Campbell looks into these four areas to show how to judge if
you are spending enough time and effort on the right areas
and why most people spend their time working in the wrong
area to achieve sustained growth in their business.

marketing mentor

Sign up to the Marketing Mentor programme – now 100% funded by Train to Gain for qualifying companies

Since launching back in April 2008, the Marketing Mentor programme has helped more than 100 small business owners make a real difference to the way that they market their companies.

It has proved to be a big success for them during these difficult economic times.

As well as the initial ideas boost of the one day seminar, the two monthly calls, advice sessions and reference notes build into a library of marketing ideas that are both practical and inspirational.

>>>

The programme consists of:

- **A one day marketing seminar** at Hothorpe Hall covering the 17 key marketing areas.
- **17 monthly phone calls** going into depth in each area.
  Calls are recorded and an MP3 audio file is e-mailed to you along with detailed notes for your future reference.
- **17 monthly shared mentoring calls** to critique any marketing materials you may have produced.
  You can also learn from other business owners using this service.
- In addition to all this, you will receive **a folder to store your materials** for future reference, a 4 CD set featuring a recording of a live low cost marketing ideas seminar, plus other bonus sections such as interviews with industry experts, authors and other bonus topics requested by popular demand.

The business building and marketing topics covered during the programme are:

- Goal Setting:
  How to get a clear sense of direction in your business – where it is heading over the next 5 years and how it is going to get there.
- Direct Mail & e-mail Marketing:
  How to generate plenty of enquiries though a successful ongoing, targeted programme.
- PR:
  How to go about generating positive stories about your business in the local / trade and national media.

- **The Sales Process**:
  How to convert more leads to appointments and more appointments into sales.
- **Brochures & Leaflets**:
  How to make sure that your brochures and leaflets are read by prospects rather than tossed in the bin.
- **Online Marketing**:
  Make sure that your website gets noticed by Google and visited by prospects.
- **Niche Marketing**:
  How to become the 'go to' company within your target markets.
- **Market Research**:
  Discover how to convert more customers, launch more successful products and keep more customers happy.
- **Referrals & Testimonials**:
  How to create ongoing systems that will create more warm leads and find out how to close more sales more easily.
- **Customer Service**:
  Find out the simplest ways of keeping your customer loyal and buying from you again and again.
- **The Phone**:
  How to make better use of one of the most overlooked marketing tools within your business.
- **The Magic Matrix**:
  Learn about a powerful way to increase your profits by creating a simple sales strategy that makes sure even a junior sales person can increase their average order value?

>>>

- **Pricing Value**:

  How to significantly decrease the chances of losing major contracts and improve the chances of extending the work you do for your best clients.

- **Networking**:

  Learn the secret techniques used by the top networkers and how to make the most of exhibitions and the people you already know.

- **Branding**:

  Learn how to improve your marketing spend by making your company and products stand out for the crowd

- **Advertising**:

  Learn how to cut your advertising budget and increase your advertising results by up to 50 fold.

- **Two Step Marketing**:

  Learn a little used idea that will ensure you always stay ahead of the competition and maintain the lead in the market place.

Because the marketing ideas covered are deemed important to help small business owners successfully grow their businesses, the programme is 100% funded if you meet the criteria laid down by the Train to Gain programme. That is: you are a business owner who employs at least four members of staff.

Call... **01858 44 55 43**
to find out more or to book your free place.